INDIVIDUATION

A Freedom from Social Oppression Anthology:
Creation of a Unique Adult Identity

Michael Holloway King, M.D.

Author of

Hide and Play Dead:
From Memoir to Real-Time Healing

And

Overcoming Oppression:
Your Guide to a New Life

PREFACE

I am pleased to present the *second* of four anthologies, or collections of narrative pieces from my first book, "Hide and Play Dead." The organizing theme for this anthology is "individuation," which is the process of finding one's truest identity. This is challenging for all persons, and may need to be repeated many times during one's life.

My experience of distinguishing myself from multiple oppressive systems was particularly difficult; I had to overcome toxic parenting, racist projections, an alternate sexual orientation, stifling educational institutions, and an incongruent career—resulting in severe post-traumatic stress disorder. However, this collection strives to make my unique process of individuation as transparent as possible. My second book, "Overcoming Oppression," allows a profound immersion experience into the nature of personality formation in the context of our largely oppressive family structures and social institutions.

Although the reading here flows with the narrative, it cannot truly compare to reading the original text with all its segments and its format as a cohesive nonfiction novel—with building suspense, balancing light or metaphysical elements, and climactic pinnacles. Footnotes have been removed, and explanatory bridging sentences inserted instead, to preserve continuity to the subject of identity formation.

You will also note that, due to my effort to heal my own post-traumatic stress disorder while writing the book, I include insightful "flashbacks" and bridging metaphors that may seem incongruent within this text, but would be easily understood in the book itself. However, they are full of innuendo and meaning in any format, whether in the original work or as discrete short stories.

The content here may be of great value for high school, college or university courses in several fields—especially the social sciences and English composition. I urge younger readers to suggest some of the following material to their professors or teachers, and for academicians to take a second look at what is revealed in these pages.

I also hope that readers will not only read the entirety of "Hide and Play Dead," but also "Overcoming Oppression." Pre-set and constricted identity models are increasingly forced upon the global masses. Feel free to visit my website and blog at www.michaelhollowayking.com, to leave comments or communicate with me directly through the blog pages, especially about the topics that this or my other works may pose. I also welcome writings from others to include in my blog and social media forums.

The narratives in this anthology are arranged by *categories* of oppression called "sequences," although there is also a loose *chronological order* for each cluster. The leitmotifs of "Hide and Play Dead" carry through all the book's stories— racism, sexuality, abusive childrearing, educational elitism, the demise of the medical field, toxic relationships, death, the meaning of life, and, especially, *neoslavery.*

Slave-based conditioning passes along transgenerational lines, and may never be healed in most family structures, unless intervention is sought. This anthology highlights the rigors of attaining a unique, personal identity rather than a slave-based, or *shame*-based personality structure. To do so within the severely oppressive black sub-group comprised of the educated bourgeoisie—the aristocracy and intelligentsia—is possibly more challenging than within any other group in America today.

- The *first* category is about the rigors of childhood, *perpetual* childhood persisting throughout adult life, within my dysfunctional family.

- The *second* category centers on adolescent rebelliousness, but within the context of America's most lofty, and most traumatizing, private high school institutions—The Phillips Exeter Academy.

- The *third* category, written in current-time and using poetic prose, shows my intensified struggle for individuation from my parents and family in late adulthood when I was writing the book.

- The *fourth* cluster deals with my career as a physician, a path forced upon me and which became unbearably oppressive as medical field fell into the hands of the business model over the past two decades.
- The *final* category brings my quest for identity to a meaningful closure.

The other anthologies in this series center on the topics of *racial identity, sexual identity*, and a metaphysical and inspirational anthology, devoted to *spiritual identity*. A workbook to accompany "Overcoming Oppression," and a guidebook for physical and mental health professionals are also forthcoming.

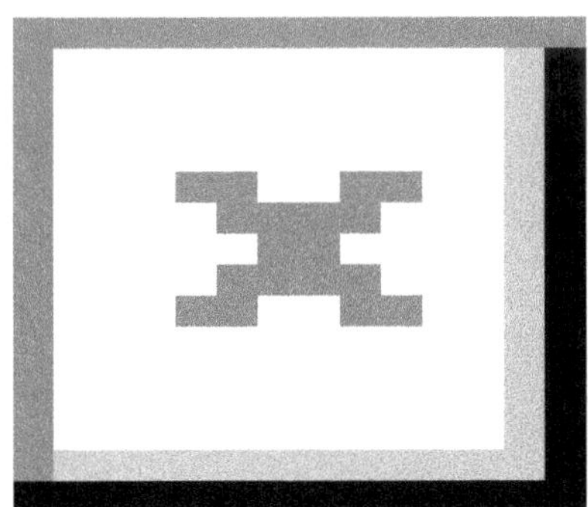

SEQUENCE ONE: CHILDHOOD IDENTITY

The trilogy of *Smothering*, *Extreme Devotion*, and *Engulfment* are representative of solipsistic, or narcissistic, childrearing practices— a psychological abuse tantamount to physical aggression.

Although widespread, such behavior was largely a derivative of the house slave mentality in my life. Two of these short narratives are set in the backdrop of racism in the late 1950's, wherein such overprotectiveness may have been understandable.

SMOTHERING

My brother, his wife, and their six-month-old baby, named Erika, have just arrived at my parent's house for a Christmas gathering. Erika is being held gently in her mother's arms and begins to cry. My mother watches the baby with growing tension, biting her lower lip; then, she bursts into angry criticism...

"*THAT'S* no way to console a baby!"

My mother pounces on Erika and snatches the baby from her mother's arms. Then she presses Erika's head hard against her bosom, burying her face into her chest. The tight embrace constricts the baby's mouth and nose. Erika stops crying. In fact, she stops breathing and she becomes slightly limp.

"Now, *THIS* is how to stop the crying!" my mother smugly proclaims.

Erika's mother is in shock. My brother's eyes are wide open, as are mine—we instantly look at each other in speechless recognition. Something ancient and familiar, something vaguely frightening from the nearly forgotten past, has just been replicated.

*

My mother never questioned the core of the transgenerational abuse pattern. She never rejected the underlying assumption that it was her

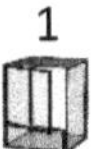

sole duty and responsibility to mold and shape the identity and the destiny, the *entirety* of her children's worlds. Indeed, she deepened the belief. She absolutely *had* to shape their worlds with extreme rigor and selfless devotion, for "raising the children" became her whole life's purpose. After all, hadn't she given up her career in music? To let them grow up *without* absolute control and strict discipline was an unthinkable and risky concept.

The methodology of *how* to raise them was never in question; she knew the techniques by heart from her own upbringing—constant vigilance and swift discipline, academic material, and implicit expectations. No coaching was needed. She only had to read a couple of books by Dr. Spock for a few more strategies.

Such limitless dedication was at first protective, although it slowly evolved into a smothering oppression. So, it happened that my mother was destined to recreate her own sad childhood and continue the transgenerational passage of slavery.

*

EXTREME DEVOTION

My parents told me that when I was about two months old, I contracted a severe case of whooping cough. I was put inside an oxygen tent in the ward of a hospital where I spent my first night completely separated from my mother. When my mother came to the hospital to check on me the next morning, she was mortified. My eyes were half open, I had a blank stare, I did not cry, and I did not respond to my mother's presence. For a while, my mother agonized as she listened to my high-pitched cough and watched me struggle for air. Suddenly, her maternal instinct erupted. She grabbed me into her arms and rushed me out of the hospital to nurse under her own care.

At the age of two, I was diagnosed with an inverted left leg. My tibia and foot turned inwards and an orthopedic surgeon decided that I should wear a rigid metal brace to rectify the problem. My mother put the brace on for the first time and took me to a playground with other children. Each time I got up to run and play with them, I stumbled and fell in tears. The brace had made me a cripple and an outcast.

My mother could not bear the sight of my struggle. She freed me immediately from the metal retainer. She held me in her arms, crying with me, telling me that I would never have to put it on again. Gradually, over the next years, I learned to master walking and running. I may have been a bit slower than my peers, but by 10th grade I became a skilled track team runner.

*

My mother's *childhood* was demolished at age three to six, when she was forced to assume the rigorous tasks of academic perfection. Then, her *adolescence* was vanquished by standards of saintly moral perfection, with no allowance for an individual identity. Down into the subconscious dungeons went a carefree, playful child and a strong and independent-minded teenager.

All the developmental learning that would have accompanied those parts of her impressionable years was so tragically incomplete that she became frustrated and depressed at an unconscionably young age. She was forced to become a replica of her father, a hard-working super-achiever, and, secondarily, fashioned by her mother to be meek and invisible for her safety.

The sense of wholeness of her Self was broken, and no contentment can come into the experience of "half a house." In *adulthood*, my mother had to "find" her missing developmental stages. She found a husband who complemented her repressed teenage years; he was awkward, ambitious and rebellious. Marriage represented a partial completion of her identity, although she quietly scorned his somewhat juvenile behavior and later realized she needed a true partner. She often humiliated my father for being *too* audacious and unreserved—it lacked class and embarrassed her.

But she still needed somebody to complete her missing early childhood *and* to be her surrogate husband.

*

A photograph of my mother and myself at age seven in 1961
While my brother and other children play in the lake, I cling to my mother "as one."

*

ENGULFMENT

My mother did not *want* to repeat the cruelty she had endured growing up, but she had no other program to use when the role of parent fell upon her. In a strange but completely predictable way, she had an urgent and desperate need to be healed through interpersonal relationships, as do all abused people.

She was completely isolated from compatible friends, living in the social vacuum of a backwards, northern city with no racial peers or equals. Her husband had abandoned her in the call for dutiful work and outside relationships. So, all she had to use for her healing were the two children that were totally "under her command."

She did not *want* to use the narcissistic programs in her head, but she had to. She did not *want* to treat her children as objects to be punished and molded for her own gratification, as opposed to independent entities to be supported and loved.

In a mysterious way, my mother rationalized that she would mitigate the abuse of forcing me into the role of being her own perpetual child and replacement husband by inserting a few gentler, add-on features, to help cancel out some of the aspects of her own painful childhood. The primary add-ons derived from her conscious agony of academic pressure and her lack of peer bonding, so she sent me the message to achieve greatness— but without pressure, and to behave impeccably— but, also, fit in with my peers.

This memoir is gripping and, for most readers, disturbing: It is about the nature of child abuse and the transmission of slave-based childrearing practices over several generations.

BRUTAL

Certain memories are *flash moments*, even though they seem to last an eternity. Others are *repeated patterns* that also seem to never end. I call the latter "telescopic memories." In the story that follows, the sequence of traumatic events occurred hundreds of times during my late childhood, with little variation.

I am feeling lonely and only my thirteen-year-old brother is at home with me. I go to his bedroom door and hesitate with apprehension before knocking. Roy, Junior's gilded poem hangs on the door in hand-painted Old English, as if from "A Midsummer Night's Dream."

> "Come into this realm of Fairyland
> Where elves and fawns and satyrs do play.
> And if thou desir'est to longly stay,
> Thy dreams shall be as the desert sands,
> Copious and vast the livelong day."

I knock softly and he does not respond. I put my fingernail in the flimsy doorknob lock, twist it and open the door. That's what we all do at home when we find a locked door. Roy is squatting on the floor, totally immersed in his squadrons of toy soldiers, scattered sheets of paper, his slide-ruler, and his new Texas Instruments calculator, which together completely fill all the space of his large room. He tells me that he is calculating the statistics, probabilities, and randomness of events in the warfare game of the toy soldiers.

Then, he shouts, "You came in without my permission! I'll *get* you for it!" Roy jumps up and lunges toward me. Frightened, I run back into my adjacent bedroom, lock my door, and put all my weight against the door to bolster it. But I feel weak and he easily forces my door open, shoves me onto my bed face down, and jumps on my back. I cannot breathe with his weight on me. Without air, I slip into a trance.

Then, he shifts his weight to my buttocks and the mind games start… "I'm reading this book. It has a *bisexual* character. Do you know what that means?"

"NO!" I gasp.

"It means he fucks *anybody*, including boys." He continues to press his buttocks onto mine. Roy's lewd allusion sends an unmistakable subliminal message. My mind whirls without conscious comprehension, but my body "gets" the taunt and freezes. It seems that he knows a secret that I'd keep from my consciousness for many years to come.

"What do you think is in a girl's *vagina*?" Roy asks.

I squeak with a barely audible voice, "I don't know."

"It's filled with *mucous* membranes. That means *buggers*. Now, you're going to eat my buggers!"

He shifts onto my chest and brings a finger to my lips. I gag in revulsion and struggle to turn my head away. Roy shifts his weight back to my buttocks and begins a rhythmical bouncing, thumping up and down on me. I feel humiliated.

Taking advantage of the partial release from his hold as he bounces, I squiggle out from under him and run to the big, sunken living room. He is chasing me in what seems to be slow motion. I grab the fireplace poker and point it defiantly at Roy. He overpowers me again, wrenching the poker from my feeble grasp and then corners me. I feel trapped and helpless as he jams the poker into my belly—not enough to leave a bruise, but just enough to show me "who's the boss." I am weak, paralyzed, and voiceless. Air only comes into my lungs when I start to cry.

Mom comes home from teaching her classes at the college. I know because I've trained my ears to detect every signal of her arrival and I've been looking out the window over and over at the sound of approaching cars to see if it's hers. I choke when she opens the electronic garage door and enters the house. I am hiding in my bedroom with all my consciousness attuned to her, *sensing* what mood she is in. The long-distance reading that I get produces even more anxiety in me.

She knocks on my door. I open it with shaky hands. "Did you boys behave yourselves while I was gone?" she asks. I start to cry and I don't want to tell her what happened, but I am unable to disobey and censor my answer. I am in a state of complete psychic surrender to her. I tattle on my brother. I expose him to my mother.

INDIVIDUATION

Mom's face slowly becomes unrecognizable. A faraway look glazes over her eyes. After a while, her face contorts with narrow, squinting eyes and her lips draw inwards, pursed hard together. Her tense body takes a deep breath in as she turns around awkwardly. Then she knocks three times at my brother's bedroom door.

DUM...**DUM**...**DUM**: A sound of foreseeable death and atonement, like a funeral march, pounds on a grand piano in my mind.

"Roy, *Junior!* Open the door! I want to speak with you!" The door opens. My mother is aghast as she scans the mess and clutter in my brother's room. She'd told him to have it all cleaned up by the time she got home. Then she begins her *interrogation*, which soon digresses into a pounding *criticism*, a machine-gun *vilification*, and then a blasting *pronouncement*.

"I'm going to have to punish you, Roy, Junior."

The captors mumble a few words:
"He'll get 150 lashes, I guess."

In a robotic trance, my mother carries a leather belt from her closet and stands in front of my brother. Roy is cringing in the far corner of his bedroom, shielding his face. Sometimes, she prefaces the whippings with: *"This* time, you'll get the *buckle* end!"

The lashing is accompanied by my mother's litany of insults and denigrations, cursing his right to live. She has lost all self-control. She will later tell me that she hallucinated her own father's voice during the beatings. 'If you don't beat your son you are a bad mother and *you* should be beaten yourself!'

The tears on my mother's face reflect the tears on my brother's, for they are united in the intimate sharing of the moment of punishment. My mother is *only* thinking about her disobedient son, and Roy is *only* thinking about his castigating mother.

I cannot stand the interminable beating. I feel guilty for having brought this fate onto my beloved brother. I break out of my nightmarish paralysis and try to intervene, to pull my mother *away from* my brother and *out of* her hysteria. I implore her to stop, tugging hard on her dress and trying to wrench the belt from her hand.

Finally, she relents. Her arm falls limp and the belt drops to the floor. She is as pale as a ghost. She turns away in silence and staggers into the master bedroom. She securely locks her bedroom door—the *only* door with a real lock in the house. There, she wails in muffled secrecy like the shrill screech of a violin string about to break.

I am now overwhelmed by an instinct to flee from the house. I think about our dog, Pip; he's been confined to the basement for hours and rarely gets outdoors to see sunlight. I release him from the smell of stool and urine that permeates his quarters and put him on his leash. He must always be walked on a leash, because he is poorly trained and tends to run away and attack neighbor's smaller pets when he gets loose.

We go up into the hills behind the house. Pip is struggling against his leash to the point of choking himself in his collar, but I am strong enough to restrain him. We trod through the snow into the invisible sanctuary of the woods. Pip discovers a steamy mound of shit from another animal, perhaps another dog. Before I can stop him, he starts to gulp down mouthfuls of the warm scat.

I am repulsed. I don't know why, *but I must beat the dog.* I am whipping him with his attached leash, shrieking, "No, Pip! NO! Bad dog! BAD DOG—" Until I see Pip lying limp on his side, whining pitifully, and then quiet. I am overcome with remorse; I've lost self-control and hurt the pet I love. How can I make it up to him? I will give him a treat when we get home.

As I return home, I sense a terrifying silence and I can "see" what is happening. With an involuntary impulse, I knock at my mother's locked door. I have my duties to fulfill. "Mom? Are you OK? May I come in?"

I hear her sobbing from her private bathroom. Then I hear the drawer, the *precise* drawer that holds both her sedatives and my father's razor blades, being pulled open.

"No, Michael. I must do this. Leave me alone now," she mutters. I hurry to fulfill my duty. There's not much time left. I know the scenario by heart. My father has shown me where the secret key to the master bedroom door is hidden; only he and I know about the key. I unlock my mother's bedroom door, slide open her bathroom door, and see her. She is crumpled into a kneeling prayer position on the floor, with a razor blade held in her right hand, hovering above her left wrist.

"I stabbed my guilty hand twenty times for the twenty questions on the test," Mom confesses.

I exhale with relief. I've arrived just in time! "Mom, you don't have to do that. I need you. I *love* you. You've done nothing wrong. Everything will be OK." I give her the messages that I know she must hear.

I escort her to her bed and she collapses as lightly as a weightless ghost. She mutters that she is a terrible mother, asks if my brother is OK, and where is my father? She hasn't seen him since 2am last night when he had to go off to deliver somebody's baby.

I call my father at his office and give him the report on his wife's status. "No, she doesn't appear to have taken any pills. She's calming down now and lying on her bed." I agree to watch her until he can break away from his patients and come home, maybe in a few hours.

I go back to my mother's bedroom and ask her if she would like a massage. She hesitates, saying she doesn't deserve one, but I insist. She needs nurturing touch as well as reassuring words. Soon I am sitting lightly on her thighs as she lies face-down on the bed. I begin to feel love and my hands instantly warm up.

I "know" just where and how to work her body's tension out. I start with her hands, which are sore from writing lectures and grading papers. Then I massage her arms and shoulders, which are taut from the horror and exertion of whipping my brother.

Then, I massage her beautiful face, which is stiff and numb from having to always perform for a racist public at her university teaching job. She is the first *black* ever hired at the college and the first *woman* in the math department—two reasons why she will be denied promotions and recognition for the next twenty-five years she will have worked there before retirement.

I massage her feet and legs, which are tired of hiding the trembling and standing proud. Then I work on her back, the scapular muscles, taut in the ambivalence of whether to reach out for support and love or pull back, inhibited.

She asks me if I want her to unfasten her bra, and I say yes and unfasten it for her. Love intermixes with shame as I do it. Now I massage her whole back and parts of her front. I feel nervous as my hands tentatively massage just the sides of her breasts. I pull down her panties and spend a long time massaging her hips and buttocks. She likes that; she is so very tense and sore there.

I "know" her body and I "know" her mind for I exist as a part of her. I can smell my mother's love now, a fragrance that is so familiar, for this entire scenario repeats several times a week, year after year. It's getting hot in the bedroom. I take off my shirt but keep my shorts on.

Finally, Dad comes home. He seems strange and irascible when he finds me finishing the massage. He stares at me sitting shirtless on his virtually naked wife and on his matrimonial bed. His look is the same as when he stared at *my* naked body the day he caught me masturbating. Suddenly I feel weak, speechless, and frozen again.

Dad promptly dismisses me from my duties and tells me to leave the bedroom. Then, sitting once again on my own bed, I listen to the crescendo of their argument. I hear my father wrestling with my mother to give her the hypodermic injection of pentobarbital that she resists. "You're being *irrational*, Estelle!" he utters in a muted shout.

After Dad leaves, my duties expand exponentially. The nightly vigil over my mother's trance-like fugue state of medicated madness begins. She will soon experience amnesia and *retrograde* loss of short-term memory. The beating of my brother will be a vague, fuzzy haze of recall, or the event will disappear from her consciousness altogether. She will also have *anterograde* amnesia and remember nothing that happens for the next four to six hours.

First, I run through the house closing and latching all the windows so that the neighbors won't hear my mother's wailing and screaming. They must not know what happens inside the walls of this prominent black family. I draw shut all the draperies, so that she will not be seen undressed as she drifts and stumbles like a phantom throughout the house and bedrooms for many hours. Sometimes she collapses naked onto her triple king-sized bed, restlessly moaning and writhing as if possessed by a demon. It's the bed where my father may spend a few hours much later tonight, at the farthest edge away from my mother and with his back turned towards her.

I am attentive to every sound and watch out for my mother's safety and wellbeing. The crash of a kitchen drawer onto the floor is identified; it's the one with all the knives and scissors. I must go gather them up quickly. The subtle rumble of a sliding glass door means Mom is about to go outside into the snow and could freeze to death. The electric garage door opens. NO! Mom must *not* drive in this state. I rush to pull her inside.

My mother opens my bedroom door many times during these interminable nighttime hours. I squelch my terror as she stumbles inside my room, nervously looking to see what's in her hands. She rants and babbles, leaning on the doorframe for support. "Where is your father? Why won't he make love to me?" she laments. "I hate my job. Why does your father force me to work? We don't need the money." She continues, "Michael, I love you so much but I'm so lonely. I have no friends here. I don't belong here."

My brother never leaves his room now, except to use the bathroom or for obligatory family meals. He has learned how to disappear behind a barricaded door, without engaging the home movie horror show. After all is once again calm, my brother will deeply repress all memory of his childhood abuse. By morning, I will pretend to be an innocent, sleeping angel, but always waiting for my door to be thrown open. And neither of us can bring visitors to the beautifully finished basement, which is empty because friends must not hear my mother's hysteria that can erupt at any moment.

*

My thoughts drift to another cherished character. There is a myth about "Ophelia," the mad woman. She drowns as an adolescent and becomes a ghost with sadness and amnesia for eternity.

> "It was the voice of mad seas, the great roar,
> That shattered your child's heart, too human and too soft...
> "The shivering willows weep on her shoulder,
> The rushes lean over her wide, dreaming brow.
> The ruffled water-lilies are sighing around her;
> At times, she rouses, in a slumbering alder..."
> *"Ophelia," Arthur Rimbaud*

With a lost childhood and adolescence, all that was left of my mother's identity was that of her own father. Of course, that was the only *permitted* identity for her to have as his obedient replica. *Her* world became *his* world, comprised of latent rage mixed with an arrogant sadness. His grandiosity blended with the grief of racial discrimination, which ultimately congealed into a sullen and wrathful frustration about life.

When all of Mom's attempts to individuate—including her choice of a passionate career in music—were summarily crushed by her father, she began to hate him. Not *consciously*, of course, but *inevitably*, due to the nature of adolescent maturation... My brother resembled and represented my mother's father— by his physical appearance, personality, and interests.

Mom's repressed rage at her father suddenly had an outlet. She projected her father onto my brother, along with her subconscious hatred and urge toward patricide. Then the inevitable happened: My mother would fragment and violently beat Roy, Junior, and then feel overwhelmed with guilt and remorse—*as if she'd attacked her own father.*

Her death wish against her own father led to morbid feelings of guilt. Such guilt demanded punishment and *that* took the form of anticipating a curse of doom, the anguish of an imaginary future disaster or some "bad news" which always awaited her. She developed a pervasive anxiety disorder based on a cynical expectation of terrible events, manifesting as a conscious pattern of incessant worrying. It also took the form of anticipating death close by her side for all the decades of her adult life, or thoughts of suicide with countless attempts over the years.

How could she have known her own future?

This short memoir contrasts material wealth with the tragedy of emotional instability, in which the latter is far more potent. A child's grand hopes are dashed by his mother's madness...

CHRISTMAS

I'm thirteen and the year is 1967. It's Christmas Eve. I'm so excited about Christmas that I hardly sleep. Dad has been up almost the whole night, setting the scene that will festoon the family with gifts. Now it's 6am and I knock on my parent's bedroom door.

"Can we go into the living room yet, Dad?" I implore.

"NO! You have to wait until 8 o'clock."

My mother asked me to choose whatever gifts I'd like over a month ago. I researched the Sears catalogue, checked out the downtown stores, and submitted a long "wish list" —with retail prices, item numbers, and location. She got furious at my excessive expectations, so I had to re-think what I *most* wanted and reduce the total price to $300. But I know that what I'll get in the end will be another $300 or more of surprises.

The thrilling moment arrives; Dad and Mom are in the sunken-floor living room. They cheerily call out to my brother and me, "YOU CAN COME IN NOW!"

I run to the twelve-foot tall Christmas tree and behold a pirate's ransom of beautifully wrapped gifts heaped up at its base, much more than I'd ever imagined. I get everything I wanted, plus many "extras." I receive a pile of educational and just-for-fun toys, games, books, and clothes. Roy, Jr. is given a magnificent huge motorized reflector telescope, programmed to track any planet or star. There are so many boxes of gifts that there is hardly room to sit and open them in the enormous living room.

My mother gets expensive jewels that will go into a safety deposit box and never be worn. My father festoons her with countless dresses, but the crowning tribute is a beautiful *brown* mink coat.... Mom is disquieted and depressed; Dad is wasting money. What about retirement? How much did he spend? And besides, she wanted the *black* fur coat.

Soon, she is berserk, bemoaning that the black coat is probably already sold and she'll *never* get the only thing she most wanted. She pulls down the Christmas tree in a ranting rage, smashing the ornaments with her feet, cursing and screaming at all of us.

My joy evaporates, the ageless terror creeps in, and my gifts become worthless; my mother has ruined the festive mood. I quickly snatch up wheel-barrel loads of my gifts before they, too, are broken, and take them away as fast as possible as I retreat down to the finished, paneled basement.

But I just look at them and cry.

Christmas is over.

This collection about the "ritual of dining" has seven short passages that carry the primary themes of the book in its simplest format.

MEALTIME

With both parents gone off to work, my childhood care is left in the hands of two, alternating, housekeeper-baby-sitter-and-cooks: Fern Rudolf and Ruby Coleman. They are like a "Mobius strip"; a ribbon strip of paper is twisted once and the ends are attached, so that one's finger traces a single line of opposite sides. Each helper spends two days working in the house, but other days, and every evening and weekend, my brother and I are left alone at home for long stretches of unsupervised hours, starting when I was seven and my mother returned to work.

"Stern Fern" frightens me. She's a spinster who'd emigrated from East Germany. She has little skill with the English language and prepares *meatloaf*—which she pronounces like an axe chopping wood:

"MIT-LOFF." Whenever Fern is our nanny, both my brother and I are on our best behavior. In fact, we whisper and slink silently from our rooms to the bathroom, and only when absolutely necessary.

Mrs. Coleman is from the deep-down South of Alabama. She's a meek and unassuming mother of thirteen children. Her unforgettable delicacy is *Chicken n' Dumplings.* Her style of babysitting is *laissez-faire.* I watch TV and read books. Roy does whatever he pleases, and his room fills up with open volumes of the Encyclopedia Britannica and the World Book, toy soldiers and pages of mathematical calculations piled up everywhere. He can do anything *except* abuse me. It is the safest time of all and I get to briefly enjoy being a child and having fun.

Ruby Coleman is also the perfect server for guests when my parents host political parties and fundraisers for the newly emerging handful of black candidates. Mrs. Coleman carries the silver trays of hors d'oevres and drinks with a quiet and unobtrusive charm.

*

The family ritualistically convenes once a day after the nannies have left or Dad has rushed home to throw together a meal, at dinnertime. Fear of the gathering obliterates my appetite. I am terrified of the family meals and I go to the table reluctantly, and only after being called several times. "I'll be right *there*, Dad!"

Both my brother and I procrastinate. Roy, Junior, is hiding on the toilet with spastic colitis. I linger in my room, finishing gluing a delicate part onto a model clipper ship.

"Come to the table *now!*" My father yells for the third time. "Your dinner is getting cold."

Finally, all four of us are seated at the breakfast nook table adjacent to the kitchen. Dad is hyperactive on diet pills, and in constant motion. He jumps up from his seat to the kitchen, and then scurries back to dump more and more food on our plates—despite our protests. For most of the meal, Dad is not sitting with the rest of us. When he does sit, he is on the phone with his answering service or a patient, and the phone is *constantly* ringing.

He talks out loud and makes mocking faces as he speaks, "Well, what *color* are the worms coming from your rectum? *White?* Oh, don't worry, Mrs. Grange. If they were *red*, you'd need medicine." He hangs up, laughing. Immediately he runs off to shovel down some food standing at the kitchen sink, out of sight and away from the table.

Mom is frowning and quiet until she says that she's having palpitations. After gulping down some Bentyl and pills for nausea and anxiety, she clutches her belly and hurries to the adjacent laundry bathroom to vomit. The gasping, gagging sounds of her retching contrast the nervous silence at the table.

Then I start laughing uncontrollably and I don't know why. I can't stop laughing until Mom stops vomiting. It masks and erases both her and her distress.

Dad checks on her and comes back to announce to Roy, Jr. and me, "She's alright. It's just that she has no gall bladder and can't digest any fat."

Then, Dad scoffs about some of his "dark-skinned, big-hipped, fat patients." Roy, Jr., hears the insult and looks down at his dark-skinned hands. He is fidgeting with his food, inspecting it and hardly eating, pushing "distasteful" bits aside. He can't stop bouncing nervously on his chair. "Sit *still* and eat your food, Roy, Junior!" my mother admonishes.

An argument breaks out between my parents. I sneak away from the table and sit on my bed with the door locked. I attune my ears, carefully listening to the heated discussion, and screening it for words that might alert me to danger.

The volcano erupts often and Pompeii is buried over and over. Dinnertime is the only time my parents interact. It's when they begin the domestic violence and my mother becomes hysterical. She screams at my father, breaks dishes and throws knives across the dining room at him. She takes some more pills and smokes a stale cigarette to calm down.

Then my father rushes off to his office, to the hospital, or somewhere far away to make a "house call." He will not return home until near dawn. I will not see him until my locked bedroom door is thrown open and the harsh overhead light is flipped on the next morning.

"Hurry up! You're *late* for school!" Dad warns, adding, "And your breakfast is getting cold." I'm *not* truly late for school—Dad just says that to make me scared enough to get out of bed and eat before he rushes off to his office, to the hospital, or away to make a house call again.

*

I dread lunchtime in the school cafeteria as much as dinnertime at home. With a full tray in my hands, I scan the crowded room for a place to sit. But students move away, suddenly "finished eating." Some slide their trays to another seat, as if to chat with a friend, and thus avoid sitting next to me. Some block the seat with personal belongings as I approach, "Oh, I'm saving the seat for a friend." Or, "It's taken."

Nobody wants me to sit next to him or her. They're in cliques to which I don't belong, they're having closed conversations from which I'm excluded, or they just ignore me in intransigent silence because I'm the Black One. I have no choice but to sit alone and without friends, or at a table with the few other rejects, usually slow learners from the special classes.

*

I've just turned seventeen and it's my freshman year at Harvard College. Meals are served in a huge dining hall called "The Student Union." 'What a strange name,' I muse. Union? I've gone through the cafeteria line and I'm holding my tray as I enter the noisy cavern that seats one thousand students, all freshmen.

I know the layout by now and I'm afraid. There are the all-white tables, divided by social class and private school affiliations; these semi-segregated tables fill most of the cavernous space. A third of the way down, on the right, is where the black students all cluster together—about eighty in total.

I have tried to sit with the blacks. They are cold and aloof toward me; my speech, mannerisms, and perhaps *something* that I just don't understand, something intangible but very real and powerful, marks me as weak. It makes them ignore me, and rush to push their trays into a tighter huddle that bars me outside.

The white tables are lonely, too. I've tried innumerable times to engage people in conversations, but with little luck. When I sit at the white tables, the blacks look over at me with rage on their faces. *'TRAITOR!'*

'Nobody wants me to sit next to him or her. They're in cliques to which I don't belong, they're having "closed" conversations from which I'm excluded, or they just ignore me in silence—because I'm the Black One.'

INDIVIDUATION

Because I'm the "*NOT* black" and the "*NOT* white" one… I've learned to walk quickly down the wide central aisle past the black tables, looking at my tray and feet so I won't stumble in front of them. Halfway down on the left is a separate round dining room. It is spacious and has windows all around its perimeter. I begin to breathe easier when I've made the sharp left angle turn and enter the special dining place.

It's the room for the international students. It's the only place I can eat without choking on my food. It is the only place where I can avoid rejection from both races—a rejection that I now accept as my lifelong fate.

*

I'm fifty-six.

My family is having dinner in a nice, new restaurant. I am seated with my mother to my right, my brother facing me sitting next to his daughter, and my father to my far right at the head of the table. It should be as it always is—predictable. It isn't. My mother opens and talks freely about her childhood memories, as my brother and I listen attentively to her stories.

"How was it growing up without any playmates, without any peers?" I ask.

"Well, at least, after age seven, I had my three cousins and when I was in high school, we went everywhere together," she replies with a faint smile.

"Who forced you to study and learn so assiduously, so precociously?" Roy asks.

"I was jealous of Narda, one of my cousins, who was four and a half and could read the newspaper. So, I asked my mother to teach me how to read at age four…and it all just flowed from there."

Somehow, the conversation leads to my mentioning the awards that I'd received in prep school. I ask my father if he remembers the awards, and that I was at the top of the class at Exeter. He admits that he'd never known anything about my achievements.

His ignorance was expected. I list my awards.

The fact that he listens to me and shows emotions, such as surprise, was a "first." But then he cuts me off; he proceeds to pull the topic over to how great a student *he* was, as the valedictorian at a small rural school. Dad insists on reciting his valedictorian speech lines from seventy years ago.

My brother engages me and gives me a card. "Why, Roy? *I'm* not a father." Rarely has a preprinted card meant something to me, but this one touches my heart:

> *There's a closeness that we share.*
> *We don't discuss it, but it's there.*
> *There's a corner of your heart reserved for someone special—*
> *The person you're so proud to call your brother.*

Roy then explains some of his revelations from doing trauma therapy, just as I am. "I've always *hated* you, Michael. I hated you because you were whiter-looking, you could pass, and you were therefore Dad's favorite. I never stopped hating you until now." My brother's gaze and his words are matter-of-fact and directed not towards me, but to my parents who appear to not hear them at all.

*

I'm fifty-seven.

Tension erupts over dinner in a restaurant with my parents when I test their openness to accept my brother's and my own recollections of the past. I try to explain why my brother feels the sting of racial prejudice, even within the family, for being darker-skinned than the rest of us.

"You know, Roy, Junior has a valid point about Dad's racist comments to him. I heard them, usually in the bathroom we boys shared. Dad would burst in and praise my *good* hair and tell Roy that his is *kinky*. So many times, Dad implied that his Roy's darker skin would block him from marriage and career possibilities, whereas I was told that I'd have my dreams come true."

My father looks furious and says the same refrain: "Why can't you just *get over* the past? Just *forget* it, because it's irrelevant now. What's your hang-up about remote events that never really happened?"

"Because the essence of your harmful behavior continues in a subtle form still today, Dad. And the events of one's childhood have a lasting and permanent effect on one's entire life. All we want is for you and Mom to admit the truth of what happened and to apologize…not 'gas lighting' and refuting our most important memories!" I explain.

Suddenly I'm getting angry, *very* angry. Nothing stings as much as victim-abuser reversal; I'm being cast as a troublemaker for even mentioning, in support of my brother, that traumatic events did happen…

"You know, they used to call Roy 'Nigger Lips' in public school," I add.

There is a wall of silent fury building around the half-eaten dinner. I glance at Mom who has been completely silent during the argument. She looks pale and mortified; she is huddled forwards with her left hand clutching her chest. Finally, she tries to speak with a voice choked by tears.

"I know more than you think I know about *everything*, Michael. *And it just hurts so very much!*" Her voice trails off mournfully into soft sobbing. In that instant, I clearly see how ardently my mother wants to completely erase and obliterate all memories and experiences of the past.

Perhaps it is her truest, deepest wish and that's why…

I reply, "No, Mom. I don't think you really know *me*."

I feel compassion for her pain, yet I am unsure *what* she knows or *thinks* she knows. It could mean anything, true or false, but something that is certainly negative about either herself or her family members. Besides, there is no apology in her words, just a plea for me to stop digging up past events.

My compassion turns back to ire as Dad begins to rant again. "Look, we gave you money, education, gifts…You *owe* it to us to let go of the past!"

He continues his familiar lecture about how I'm emotionally handicapped and all my problems are my own fault: They were great parents or nearly so… They gave their sons everything, without any gratitude ever returned… Their two children have had an *easy* life compared to their hardships…

I *SNAP*. I stand up abruptly from the unfinished meal in the middle of the restaurant. I throw on my coat and brusquely storm off, leaving my parents both embarrassed and shocked.

MICHAEL HOLLOWAY KING

SEQUENCE TWO: ADOLESCENT IDENTITY

EXETER, PARTS ONE AND TWO **is a versatile couplet that addresses the mindset of adolescence and educational elitism.**

EXETER: PART ONE

Weakness saps my body as my parents disappear, driving away from Exeter, New Hampshire, and heading back to Erie, Pennsylvania, one thousand miles away. I drift inside the mysterious two-towered Soule Hall to set up my room. 'You're on your own now,' I ponder. I've just turned fifteen years old.

I know that I have arrived at the top-ranked, private high school in America, The Phillips Exeter Academy—the oldest, the toughest, and the loftiest education possible. Exeter already had a reputation for being an austere and cold place whose spirit books and films have sought to convey, but none can ever capture.

I watch those who arrive in limousines from Manhattan and those with bejeweled escorts, the scions of the most affluent and famous and powerful families in the country. I know that my public-school education is leagues behind my classmates' years of private schooling and tutors.

I'd passed the "Secondary School Admission Test" with very high scores. Only the brilliant are allowed into this exclusive club, where excellence is the norm and where I must go on... *"To achieve the nearly impossible, seemingly without effort."*

I unpack my two triple-button sports coats and my collection of six ties that I must wear to every class and to the dining hall. I read the long list of rules and regulations with stipulations that, if breached, would lead to immediate probation or expulsion:

- Not to be seen in a moving vehicle without prior approval from the Dean.

- Not to arrive at class later than one minute and each episode of tardiness will be reported to the Dean who will issue a probation order on the third episode in any given semester.
- Not allowed to ever leave the classroom without explicit permission under any circumstances or an immediate probation order will be issued.
- Three probation orders in one year will warrant immediate expulsion from the Academy.

And not allowed a single wasted minute! Daily quizzes begin immediately and unpredictably. There are weekly exams, which are harder than at most graduate-level universities. Books must be read and digested in a couple of days, immediately learning to write in the precise style of the author. There are six- to ten-page typed essays three times a week.

Perform under pressure or leave. I would soon feel a constant anxiety that curdles my breakfasts. Lights out at 9pm for "preppies," 10pm for "lowers," 11pm for "uppers," and unsupervised for "seniors." I'm a mere "lower."

The rituals begin; the tower bell rings, ATTENTION! Every ring of the bell has a specific command associated with it—the *detested* bell that one night we would engineer to remove with an elaborate system of ropes and pulleys, and then hide it in the Exeter woods under branches and leaves.

With my tie wrapped tight around my neck, I scurry with other boys along a dream-like New England autumn landscape. I trot nervously past breathtaking Georgian and Tudor-Stuart buildings covered in ivy, up marble stairs, and into the morning assembly hall—and then to class after class for two terrifying years.

There will never be more than eight students in a class, gathered around a lustrous two-ton hardwood oval table: The famous "Harkin's Table" legacy. Head count: nine hundred fifty boys and three hundred teachers, when expert consultants were counted in. All the teachers are selected from the best of the best.

Everything is the best of the best…

Modeling British public schools by tradition since 1783, teachers are to be called by the title: "Master." I cringe at the thought, and then I smirk; my first English teacher's last name is "Bates." My math teacher smells of morning vodka and is too touchy-feely and intimate with his boys. But nobody cares; he'd written the textbooks used in the honors classes of public schools nationwide.

Obligatory afternoon athletics in the ultra-modern gym complex with two hockey rinks seating six hundred, two full indoor gymnastic stadiums, an indoor cage for track, lacrosse and baseball, an eight-lane championship pool seating four hundred fifty viewers, nineteen all-weather tennis courts, fourteen squash courts with one hundred-seat galleries, four basketball courts, a magnificent stone coliseum for football, the boathouse...

Exeter: the ultimate splendor and specter, boasting a solid endowment of nearly a billion dollars. I arrive during a fundraiser for twenty million dollars to construct the spiral glass library listed as one of the ten architectural masterpieces in America.

Twenty million dollars spent in 1970 for a school that already had... "You can always do better."

The Academy building and belfry at the Phillips Exeter Academy

My first roommate is dismayed to discover a Negro is sharing equal space with him. "My nanny was black and that's the only one I've ever known." Then he adds, "You people are genetically weak and that's why Africa was so easy to conquer." He sweats cold rage when I beat him at tennis, and then the blood vessels of his temples appear on the verge of bursting when I try to coach him from flunking math.

Another kid in a neighboring suite lets me see his fancy new stereo equipment. "My father produced all the Beatles movies. You're wearing purple bell-bottoms. Only black people dress like that." I remind him of how the Beatles dress.

The rumor spreads among the teachers that I am Martin Luther King's nephew. Only *famous* people belong at Exeter, so I let it slide. White classmates stay aloof: they know I'm just black and ordinary. When the movie "A Separate Peace" is filmed at the school, a memo goes out that blacks must stay outside of the filming area "because it is not consistent with the 1950s period in which the film is based." I am used to racism and I have my ways to avenge it.

The shame of abandonment I'd felt for being "not white" in Erie takes on another dimension; I discover that I am also "not black." The anticipation of finally knowing other blacks erodes into this new and disappointing level of ostracization. After my first year at Exeter, I ask the president of the support group for the fifty non-white students, the "Afro-Exonian Society," why I'd not been invited to a single meeting. "Because you're *Pakistani*," he replies.

Whatever shame I'd felt in Erie would be transformed by Exeter for years to come. Race would still provoke a deep, primordial anxiety that would resurface often enough; it would always be linked to my "dirty" brown skin and my genetic stigma. It would remain a factor in my struggle for identity, but recede a bit into the background.

My new peers did not have a middle-class provincial mentality and few were truly racist. They were "citizens of the world," members of a distinct group that had been exposed to international travel and liberal educations, by grace of money, class, and privilege.

My survival at Exeter now depended on other factors. Fortunately, the new stratification largely nullified external social status. Inside the confines of the Academy, we were all elite members of the intelligentsia. Here, rank was determined by scholastic achievement and *only* academic performance mattered. Criticism by teachers who had been granted complete and unquestionable ruling authority came to signify a threat to our future and, literally, a threat to survival at Exeter and beyond.

*

EXETER: PART TWO

Professeur Jacquard is an old French aristocrat whose personal history is an irrelevant mystery. All that matters is that he has taught at Exeter for a *very* long time. He does not speak a single word of English during my first year of foreign language instruction. He quickly grades my first "surprise quiz," then drops my exam paper down on the middle of the oval table for all to see: D-minus. I've never gotten less than a rare A-minus in Erie.

Scorching tear-gas gushes of terror accompany my appeal for help after class. I promise to meet privately with him several times a week to catch up with the other seven students, all of whom have already studied French for at least three years in private schools, and several have homes in France or travel there often.

Professeur Jacquard begins to show gentle, even paternal, warmth toward me as I make earnest progress. My dreadful anxiety begins to transform into reverence for my teacher. I want to please him like no teacher I've ever had before or would ever have after. He corrects my pronunciation until it is flawless. Soon I am reciting lengthy verses of poetry by Rimbaud from memory. Within a few months, I'm reading Sartre, Camus, Voltaire, and then Proust. By the third semester, I'm writing scripts for plays in French, modeling 18th century classics, such as Molière.

After four semesters, I am given the annual French Award for the entire Academy. Then, I will be placed in *seventh*-year French, or the 2nd year graduate-school level, at Harvard College. By skipping five years, I will mingle with students who had graduated from the Sorbonne.

*

To achieve a state of constant performance anxiety and relentless angry competition, certain age-old conditions were implemented at Exeter.

Self-acceptance is *denied.* Exeter lacked all elements of kindness as the students were completely subjugated under the whip of forced achievement. A terrifying pressure to perform engulfed us all equally, and the voracious dragon had no boundaries or mercy. There was no reprieve from expectations. To stop and enjoy my achievements, or to rest on my laurels as finally being "good enough," was taboo.

All imaginable hours of the week were consumed by studies. Like my peers, I was prodded and driven relentlessly towards a limitless better. To do well in a class meant that I would be selected for a more exclusive class and subjected to even *higher* expectations, and the cycles of heightened competition would begin all over again. Sleep deprivation was inevitable and worth the risk of being caught with the desk lamp on after "lights out"; writing, reading, and cramming for the next day's ordeal *had* to be done.

Relaxation is *denied*. Barrages of criticism and humiliating debates with teachers constantly put one's ego in jeopardy. There was, in theory, some free time on Saturday after 4pm through Sunday night, a freedom limited by weekend assignments and preparation for Monday's exams. Still, with bated breath and ardent anticipation, I awaited the tiny bit of weekend freedom. It provided a momentary respite from the daily grilling and tests, a thirty-six-hour cease-fire.

Peer group relationships are *denied*. In the all-boy Academy, there was a certain subtle innuendo of bonding, but it was too vague to define and only happened in glimpses or rare moments. Mutual competition and, even more, sheer lack of time, obliterated interpersonal friendships. I felt the same loneliness as in Erie, but it was a sentiment that was shared equally with my classmates.

The student lounge in my dorm, Soule Hall, was home for some exhausted peers gathered in solitary dissociation, watching TV during short evening breaks when TV time was allowed. There was also a game table in the lounge—a shuttle-ball whose levers were slammed in unrepressed fury. Bang! Bang! Until the ball was knocked so hard that it flew off the table onto the floor. Crack! Crack! *ROLL…*

Reciprocity is *denied*. The ordinance was to surrender and sacrifice everything for achievement. In exchange, I was rewarded not by something precious and human like *love*, but rather by the empty and intangible substance of grades, honors, and awards.

THAT WAS OUR HEAVEN.

I would alchemically convert D's into A's like water into wine; a set of A's converted into top-class ranking with "Highest Honors" and coveted prizes; then, class rank and accolades converted into freedom from Exeter with early entry into Harvard College directly from the 11th grade.

AND THEN, THERE WAS OUR HELL.

The terror of getting caught for something warranting expulsion from the Academy came to signify a sentence much worse than death. Several of my peers attempted suicide; to lie down on the main street at night and wait for a *vehicle* to come, or to overdose on drugs and wait for *salvation* to come—these were better than being expelled.

There was one firm and solid rule that automatically received the death penalty of expulsion: illegal drug use or any alcohol consumption.

I discovered another place, beyond the main floor TV lounge, where *other* students could spend free time. It was called "The Butt Room." The cramped dungeon was where select students could gather to smoke cigarettes, with parental consent.

One day, I ventured down the narrow dark stairway and into a dense cloud of various types of burnt materials. Sometimes it was a paper or an exam that had earned a bad grade, and sometimes it was a letter from one's parents. Sometimes it was marijuana or hashish, concealed by tobacco, with a fan sucking the smoke out through the little basement window—the Butt Room door closed, and someone standing guard to block the uninvited.

I craved membership in *anything* other than the pathetic loneliness of solitary achievement; my instincts pleaded for human bonding. I knew nothing about drugs, but I drifted down to the Butt Room more and more often. Gradually, I "heard" and "knew" that therein existed an admission ticket to peer bonding.

I was cautiously taken through the stages of initiation into this clandestine club. After six months of guard service and sworn secrecy, I'd be permitted to participate in the only ritual of interpersonal connection that Exeter offered: the passing of the joint. When the hand-rolled "cigarette" was finally passed to me, I knew that I was now both an accomplice and a criminal within the first peer group of my entire life—*and I felt honored.*

This trilogy— *Budding Buddies, Busted,* and *Punished*—is about adolescent drug use and my parent's reactions; my mother's cunning and murderous hysteria, and my father's incestuous feelings towards me heighten the story.

BUDDING BUDDIES

Soule Hall is the notorious headquarters of the drug trade at the Phillips Exeter Academy. The sultans of marijuana, hallucinogens, and alcohol reside in the two lofty suites at the top of both spiral staircase towers. The turret tops have come to symbolize for me a steep climb and a risky ascent toward peer acceptance and bonding.

The penthouse of one tower is where two post-graduates are roomed: Ned and Jerry. They returned after their senior years to try to pass flunked courses. If they pass, they'll graduate and still get into a good college, but not into the Ivy League, and they don't give a damn about it.

Both come from extraordinary wealth and are rebellious against the control of their families and of Exeter. They've chosen an identity of dissociation and sadness: dropouts. That means *hippy* in 1969 and the two young men are paragons of the "free-*something* movement." They wear frilled leather jackets and dirty blue jeans that reek of dope. They ride expensive motorcycles, play electric guitars, and have frequent female visitors.

Ned dies in the early 1980s in a motorcycle accident.

The penthouse of the other tower is Timothy's room; he's in my class. His father is a senior diplomat in the Far East. "Diplomatic immunity" means that Timothy can smuggle certain exotic treasures from the Orient back to Exeter: bricks of oil-permeated resins to share with his devotées. We listen to firesign theater records over and over as Timothy fantasizes living in a Taj Mahal made of hashish, a variation on the themes of gingerbread or ice cream houses.

Timothy befriends me through drugs and ushers me into my final and full initiation. Every weekend allowable, he requests permission from the Dean to visit his grandmother in Boston, along with a few select classmates on the invitation list. Every weekend, he and his coterie of six friends return from Boston with new drugs. I feel as proud of his invitation to go to Boston with him as I do when I achieve the top grades, "Highest Honors."

Timothy's grandmother's house is unlike anything I've ever seen. It's a six-story brick townhouse on Beacon Hill, in the very heart of the ruling "Boston Brahmin" territory. Weekends, most servants are gone and Timothy and his friends can have the rooms on the 6th floor. Due to her age, his grandmother rarely climbs up past the 4th floor and only one butler poses a risk. There, on a Sunday in February 1970, I finally fully "inhale" and feel the power of marijuana.

About this time, *other* sentiments are beginning to stir again, deep inside me. I dimly sense that the passing of the pipe from one boy's lips to mine suggests something more to me than to most of my peers.

INDIVIDUATION

Boundaries palpably loosen and dissolve as we gather in a circle, shoulder-to-shoulder and thigh-to-thigh. Being stoned and dissociated fosters a drawing even *closer* together, into a merging that is almost intimate in our shared state of altered consciousness. I assume my feelings pass unsuspected, but I fear that, perhaps, I have a biological marking, a subtle "signature," that other males can detect on some level.

Our cluster of six stoned boys is called downstairs for tea and sherry. It is served in fine porcelain cups and crystal glasses. "Just a *little* bit of sherry, mind you! You're still boys!" his well-dressed grandmother warns us with poise.

On Sunday, we prepare to return by private coach back to Exeter. Before leaving, the pipe is passed many times, relishing our last moments of freedom and bonding. As I walk down the mansion's stairs floor-by-floor, the walls begin to shift from squares to circles and the crystal chandeliers emit a golden haze. After a seemingly very long time, I arrive at the 2nd floor landing; the shape and color of the space around me is now like the inside of a pulsating pumpkin. I'm suddenly petrified and lose my balance, holding onto the mahogany railing and struggling to get down to where Timothy's grandmother stands bidding Timothy and "his nice friends" a cordial farewell.

Outdoors in the deep slush, frigid cold, and falling snow of a Boston winter, I ask Timothy, "Am I going to die?"

Timothy's behavior becomes uncontrollable from drug abuse a year later. I visit him at his parents' home in Georgetown, near Washington, DC, and accompany him on a deadly spree of reckless driving without a license. Timothy speeds wildly about the Capitol in a family van that was taken without permission. He is zigzagging across the lanes, crashing into parked vehicles, ripping off car doors, tipping into a wall––but not getting caught. I am gripped by an unimaginable panic, which will creep into my nightmares forever since.

I ask Timothy, "Are *we* going to die?"

The next year, Timothy joins an evangelical Christian group.

Juan Bernardo is uncharacteristically friendly toward me. He comes from Colombian aristocracy and has learned English in private schools in Bogotá. He speaks voluminously, but with a heavy Spanish accent and a limited vocabulary. But somehow, he knows all the words describing the cruder aspects of copulation. He spends hours lingering in my single, private room, sitting on a chair and telling me fantastic stories of his sexual encounters with horny nuns. Then, he begins to sit on my bed next to me.

I feel more anxious with Juan Bernardo than I feel in any of my honors classes. My lack of mental constructs, images, or role models impedes all action. Juan Bernardo even flies to Erie with me for a fall holiday, forsaking a return to South America. If only I'd understood....

Juan Bernardo dies in the early 1980s during the height of the AIDS epidemic.

*

BUSTED

I never wanted to hurt my parents; I only wanted their approval and love. Yet, when it came to my using drugs or drinking alcohol, we were at odds. I'd just asked them for permission to smoke cigarettes so that I could deepen my inclusion in the Butt Room clique under the cloak and cover of a "reason" to be spending time there.

They did not give me permission to smoke. Instead, my parents made a special surprise trip to Exeter only a few weeks after I'd gone to Timothy's lair at his grandmother's house.

Somehow they knew...

My mother is sitting on my bed in the dormitory room while my father is outside, scouting around Soule Hall. She'd asked for a private *tête-à-tête* with me. I haven't missed my parents at all, although they seem to have missed me terribly. The path along which my identity is forming is entirely separate from their world. What could *they* know about Exeter?

"Michael, my son. You're almost a man now, aren't you?" I am standing with my back toward my mother, looking out the window and two floors down at my parents' parked car, just letting her words pass by.

My mother continues in a muted whimper, "I'm *proud* of you. You seem to have adapted so well here. You've amazed us—Highest Honors! Are you the first black student to ever get Highest Honors?"

"Yes, Mom." I turn and look at her face. Her eyes seem to be imploring and exploring at the same time.

"I know you're a man, but do you remember how you used to sit on my lap when I read stories to you as a child?"

"Yeah."

"It may be silly of me, but I'd really like it if you'd come closer to me and sit on my lap, just one last time. I miss you so very much!"

INDIVIDUATION

I hesitate. I feel suspicious and anxious. She wants me to pretend to be a three-year-old again? Yet, I also feel a powerful pull toward her, to do what she wants, to try to make her happy, just like I always did when I lived at home. What could be the risk?

I am sitting on her lap, with my hands pushing down on the bed to protect her from my full weight. I might crush her legs and I don't want to hurt her. Her arms are hugging me close to her bosom in a desperate embrace. I shift my weight again, pulling away from my mother's chest. It's *too* close. "Michael, you'll never know how much I love you," she whispers in my ear.

Then she begins to recite by memory my favorite childhood poem, "The Walrus and the Carpenter." I always identified with the naïve, gullible oysters that were lured into the devouring mouths of their predators. Just like when I was a child, she emphasizes certain passages of the poem....

> **"The time has come," the Walrus said,**
> **"To talk of many things:**
> Of shoes—and ships—and sealing-wax—
> Of cabbages—**and Kings**—
> And why the sea is boiling hot—
> And whether pigs have wings."
>
> "A loaf of bread," the Walrus said,
> "Is what we chiefly need:
> Pepper and vinegar besides
> Are very good indeed—
> Now, if you're ready, Oysters dear,
> We can begin to feed.'
>
> "But not on us!" the Oysters cried,
> Turning a little blue.
> **"After such kindness, that would be**
> **A dismal thing to do!"**
> "The night is fine," the Walrus said,
> 'Do you admire the view?"

I am losing myself, lulled and swayed by nostalgic words as she finishes the poem by Lewis Carroll...

> "O Oysters," said the Carpenter,

> **"You've had a pleasant run!**
> **Shall we be trotting home again?'**
> But answer came there none—
> And this was scarcely odd, because
> They'd eaten every one.

I am drifting back in time. I feel lighter and weaker as I merge with my mother's voice. My boundaries are now obliterated.

"So, Michael. I know young people need to explore the world. I know many will experiment with things…like drugs. Look at me and tell me—*Have you tried marijuana?*"

I look at her entreating, loving eyes and I cannot lie. "Yes, Mom. I've tried it." Instantly, her pupils constrict into a cold stare and her mouth contorts into a demonic snarl. Her *pull* shifts into a violent *push* and I am thrown to the floor.

My mother is shrieking, "You're damned! I hate you! You're lost now. You're going to kill yourself on drugs and that's a horrible way to die. *I should kill you now and take you out of your misery!*"

She lunges at me with her fingers deformed into talons, scratching at my face. An hour later, she will walk in an aimless daze without a coat or shoes in the freezing streets of Boston. She will try to get run over as she stops rush-hour traffic and vehicles swerve around her, honking their horns furiously.

My father will not leave the hotel room to bring her back to safety. Instead, he commands me: "Go get her before she kills herself! It's all your fault!" I will go get her, alive but not well. I don't care what she says or does anymore. I hate her.

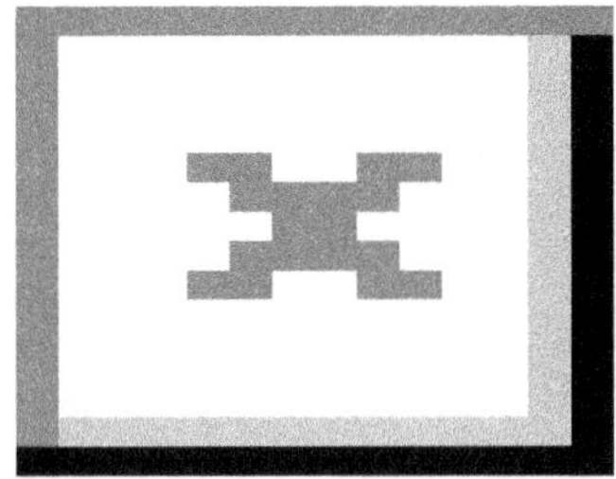

*

PUNISHED

It's my second year at Exeter and I've flown home to Erie for Christmas break. In my heavy fake-fur coat is an ounce of hashish concealed in the lining through a little hole in the right pocket. I have written in my diary about being stoned, taking LSD and other hallucinogens, and being so high that I was scared. My diary is mixed with matching binders of class notes locked in a suitcase.

The day after my arrival, my father calls me into the laundry room, far from my mother who is resting in her bedroom at the opposite wing of the house. I stand a few feet in front of my father who is looking down at something that he is holding hidden in his cupped hands.

"Michael. Your good mother found a hole in your coat pocket. She will sew it for you. Then she found something wrapped in aluminum foil, which she unwrapped. She thought it was chocolate and felt sorry for you for being so hungry that you've got to take chocolate around. *I've read your diary,*" Dad says solemnly.

My father then opens his hands to show me the hashish. He lifts his head up and I see tears falling down his face. I have never seen my father cry before.

"I'm going to have to punish you, Michael." Dad has *never* physically punished my brother or me.

"Just *how* do you plan to do that, Dad? Give the hash back to me!"

Dad pushes me and wrestles me to the floor. I fight back and we're equally strong now. Tears become laughter at the absurdity of the attempted punishment. Suddenly he relaxes all his muscles and lets his full body weight just lie on top of me, with his head next to mine for a long time.

Too long…

He sighs and then he holds me in a tight embrace, lifting his head to gaze lovingly into my eyes—face-to-face. His lips are close to mine, *too* close…

The look on his face is the same as when he caught me masturbating and massaging my mother. I shove him off and go to my room.

The following story has a wry sense of humor, capturing an adolescent's insecure arrogance, heightened by elitism, and propensity to "hate" authority figures.

KEEP RUNNING

Elitism roughens one's soul like acid. It provides the intoxicant of Narcissism to all who imbibe its vapors. But adolescence is all about angry arrogance, anyway. Exeter just magnified it many-fold.

It's time for the big track meet: Exeter Academy versus its archrival and "brother school," Andover Academy. I'm to compete in the one-mile race. I don't like the longer runs; I do much better sprinting in the thousand-yard dashes. Somehow, I never learned to pace myself for anything long-distance. I typically get off to a great start, ahead of the pack; then, I maintain a good lead, but it saps my energy. The *last* stretch is when I need reserves to slam on the accelerator, but I'm too exhausted by then.

My coach's name is "Bucky." He's a fat slob and I'm convinced that he's a racist. In his mind, I bet he thinks, 'King's skinny and nervous. He has long legs and he's black. Therefore, he *should* be a winner.' Rumor has it that Bucky graduated from Exeter in the distant past. When he's not the coach, he's the short-order cook in the Exeter Grill.

He fries hamburgers and fixes up coleslaw. No graduate of Exeter would be stuck as a cook!

I can't respect Bucky. I don't *like* him, either. He yells and insults the runners, as if that were motivational. He's never taught me a thing. On the field or in the grill, he's always grumpy and grouchy. He lacks the art of intellectual discourse. Another rumor claims that Bucky is just a *Townie*. That's the derisive word used to refer to the townsfolk in Exeter—a bunch of nothings, numbering a few thousand, all "village idiots": clerks, gas station attendants, and menial workers…

The "Townies" hate and envy the "Preppies."

Another rumor is that Townie girls are easy to lay because they're stupid and impressed by a great Exonian. Then, the girl's Townie boyfriend gets jealous and picks a fight with one of us. There've been some skirmishes between public high school students and my boarding school peers. So, it's against the Academy's *unwritten* rules: Preppies and Townies are not supposed to mix.

When Bucky gets excited, he starts shooting his stupid pistol wildly in the air, as if to give more punch to his shouts. "KING! MOVE THOSE SKINNY LONG LEGS FASTER!"

POP! POP! POP: as Bucky shoots the blanks into the air.

Some of my classmates found dead ducks along the Exeter River. I think we can stuff them in the overhead netting of the enclosed track stadium. All I need is a rope to pull open a jimmy-rigged hatch and dump the dead ducks on Bucky's head the next time he shoots his damn pistol like that. I can just imagine his face with half-rotten ducks plopping down on his wrinkled, bald scalp!

I hate track. *We're intellectuals!* Brains and brawn don't mix. That's why Andover usually wins; they're only ranked *third* among the best schools. We're *first* by a long way. Tennis or squash are much more appropriate than track. There's more intelligence involved. One of my classmates prefers to water ski. He said that blacks aren't good water skiers because they have a denser body mass than whites and can't swim as well.

That pissed me off! I retorted, "Well, *maybe* they can't generally afford swimming pools or yachts, don't you think?"

I'm doing my last warm-ups. The viewing bleachers around the large indoor stadium are packed with people that I don't know. Viewers make me nervous; if they're Townies, they're just like the people in Erie. They'll only see my skin, not my Highest Honors grade-point average. It's creepy when white strangers' eyes are looking at me.

If I think about them, I instantly lose my steam and my breath. I wonder why that happens.

OK, it's time to get in position.

"Get ready…Get set…*GO!*"

POP! POP! POP!

I'm doing the usual, looking good and well ahead of the pack.

This time I'm going to reserve some energy for the last lap…

They're looking at me from the *bleachers* and that reminds me of something from when I was a little kid—Damn! Thinking slowed me down, and now I'm trailing behind two Andies…

OK, I've caught up and it's the last lap.

ZOOM…

I'M DOING IT! I'M IN THE LEAD!

I don't see the little rock on the course because my attention is riveted on the finish line. My left foot catches the rock, my ankle twists and snaps as I fall face down eating the dirt. I can't believe my bad luck! I try to get up but my ankle hurts so bad I can't even stand. I'm ten feet away from the finish line on all fours like a fool.

Bucky comes over to me and starts kicking my legs. "You got to finish, KING!" Bucky shouts. "Get up and finish the race, KING! No excuses, KING! KEEP RUNNING, KING!"

POP! POP! POP! The blanks seem to explode at my ankle like a white man shooting at an Indian's feet to make him dance. Bucky keeps kicking me as if I'm a *mule* and I want to bite his fat ankle like a rabid dog. I crawl the ten feet to the line and then I just lie there in so much pain that I'm crying. Finally, someone brings me ice and crutches.

I hate Bucky.

"KEEP SWIMMING!"

"KEEP DANCING!"

"KEEP RUNNING!"

THE DRUMBEAT IS SCALDING HOT

SEQUENCE THREE: ADULT IDENTITY

Admittedly, this is a psychological and expository excerpt that relates and summarizes my dilemma and the nature of solipsistic engulfment. It places my mother's refusal to allow me to excel or to grow up within the context of my IQ.

THE OMEN AND THE CURSE

My mother knew that I was marked with a genetic advantage and that both her sons would be extraordinary: unique, academically gifted, and born with a potential for greatness—just as she had been. My mother knew, almost as if it were an *ominous prophecy*, that she contained inside her pregnant belly the essence of greatness. And she hated it.

"I grew feeling the sperm of greatness like a sore in my heart and abdomen."
[From my mother's diary, written when pregnant with me inside her womb]

When I was five years old and my brother was seven, Mom suddenly had to know. She took us to a psychologist to test our IQs. She looked maudlin and distraught when she later told me the results: "One of you has an IQ well above 180, which is the Einstein level of genius. The other was just a few points lower."

She refused to say which of her sons got the higher score, but I just assumed it was my brother. I'd been so frightened during the testing that I trembled and rushed through the questions in record time, to get away as quickly as possible.

Just as my mother was forced to educate herself and achieve the extraordinary in academic studies by dint of her father's subtle, yet merciless pressure, her insistence that I receive the best education in America resulted in the same merciless pressure for me to achieve the extraordinary that she had attained.

My mother valued education highly as a transgenerational rebel slave tradition. She endorsed the move to the suburbs of Erie, to allow her children to attend the best public schools within the city. Thereafter, my life experience was quite distinct from that of my parents; new variables appeared that confounded their simplistic, antiquated reasoning based on their own pasts.

My liberal education in elite schools, especially Exeter and Harvard, trained me to challenge authority, to think independently, and to creatively integrate a critical meta-analysis of things, people, and events into a big picture. Unlike public school and most college curriculums, mere rote memorization and the acquisition of ordinary skills were largely omitted. Essentially, I learned to be an iconoclast. I was cultivated to expect independence and individuation, and even to seek a bit of egotistical reward or "narcissistic supply."

So, I followed my mother's prophecy of academic greatness. By age twenty when I graduated from Harvard College, I had proved I was unique, even outstanding, and I could do extraordinary things. But *this* was not the obstacle to "fitting in" with my peers; I was educated in consummately prestigious institutions and everybody I knew was *also* extraordinary.

I now realize that there was more than an omen in my mother's mind: There was also a *curse* cast on me. My mother's prophecy had a clause that was a repressive edict; she revoked her permission for me to manifest "greatness" completely. She declared that her offspring should not be allowed to manifest this terrible gift…

"My children will NOT inherit the spark and drive I possessed…
And they will NEVER do the extraordinary."

Both my parents colluded, for different reasons, to close and lock the door to my true destiny. I was shamed, ridiculed, and mocked whenever I did something extraordinary. And there was absolutely no encouragement to be unique. My mother mandated that I should be ordinary and fit in to correct her wretched childhood isolation from peers as a child prodigy.

Paradoxically, my parents expected saintly moral perfection and extraordinary academic performance, and then they punished me when I attained it. In an exact replication of slavery, praise was nonexistent in my home, and aloofness, disrespect, and criticism were constant—no matter what I did.

To be unique, but pass as common, was an oxymoron and an impossible task. It simply meant that my individuation as a free entity had to be blocked at some point, and that my gifts and achievements had thenceforth to be discarded or concealed. That is exactly how my mother lived her life starting with her father's refusal to allow her to become a concert pianist at age sixteen. Then, when she moved to Erie, her gifts invoked envy and risk in a racist and unsophisticated milieu.

I have held a long-standing and deep-seated rage at my parents' betrayal that peaked at age twenty. I felt besieged by their assault on my individuation, as I tried to hold shut my castle gates against the ramrods of one of the greatest abuses possible: mandatory falsification of one's identity.

THE OMEN AND THE CURSE ARE VOIDED: I CAN BE EXTRAORDINARY AND FIT IN WITH OTHER EXTRAORDINARY PEOPLE.

The following couplet consists of two juxtaposed pieces of poetic prose, with the metaphors of "hands" and "lightning." I use vivid imagery to depict an adolescent's or traumatized adult's struggle for identity. The second piece may be re-read after reading "Career Identity Foreclosure," which opens the next section on "career identity."

THE HANDS

The tension of my ambivalence is mounting. There are hands with voices that pull me back: You're wasting your time! There is no way out. Stay in your cave.

It's my first day in boarding school. I see my mother's tear-soaked face turned back to look at me in the passenger window as my father drives her off, leaving me waving good-bye on the steps of Soule Hall. She is wailing, "NO! Not my *second* child! Don't take him away from me too!" I am wrenched from her arms to be sold into slavery, sold "down the river" into other hands.

Then, too, there are hands that want to suppress the book. Each voice lauds the content, yet urges omission of issues based on their own fear and shame.

"Don't mention pornography!"

"The part about massaging your mother is very intimate!"

I argue with the voices. I am digging myself out of this cave. **Earth and rock must yield!**

I have a little hole in the wall of rocks now and I can see the tunnel and shaft ahead of me. I can smell fresh air as the critical mass of trauma becomes unearthed. I just need to dislodge these next boulders to free my ensnared body from captivity. Then I will venture further into the subterranean labyrinth of my subconscious as I seek the light of freedom above.

There has been a shift in my conscious recall from birth to age fourteen. None of the traumatic memories intrude anymore and I can see the full picture of my early development, my "impressionable years." I will now re-live being yanked from the quicksand of the provinces to the treadmill of the most prestigious education possible in America for my "formative years." I will tackle the worlds of achievement and Narcissism, of geniuses and Brahmins.

"The spark and drive I possessed will not be inherited by my children and they will never do the extraordinary... And I do not care at all."

There are other hands with different voices that pull me down: The past is rotten compost. There is no use for it. You are digging your grave. I scrape and scratch with my bleeding fingers and broken nails to break the chains like a rebel slave shackled in the cargo hold of a ship. The constriction of my identity by external pressure is heightened by recent interactions with my parents. "You just have to realize that...." they say, over and over.

I argue with the voices. I am digging for hidden treasure! **Earth and rock and chains must yield!**

I am aware that the next chapter of my life will reveal the forces of defiance and conformity that shaped my social identity. I will see the new identities of "elite" and "gay" as they amalgamate with "black." I will be ripped into three, then four parts of Self.

There are also hands with voices that pull me forward: You are creating a mandala. It only *appears* to be a jigsaw puzzle. A portal to another world is open for you.

I have survived a shipwreck and a tempest has blown my lifeboat onto an island where I can get fresh water. But provisions are scarce. My boat has holes of unchanged habits in its hull that need repair. I do not know if it is seaworthy.

I can just barely make out a silvery dot on the horizon across the vast ocean of my subconscious. The Silver City is my destiny. I have no sails or turbine to propel my boat through the water, but the sea appears calm and the waves appear favorable. I believe I can paddle my boat there—even though I will have no respite from now on. Keep swimming! Keep digging! Keep rowing!

I do not argue with the voices. Spark and drive ignite wind into fire that blazes in my soul.

Earth and rock and chains and water must yield!

Phylogeny replicates ontogeny. The prior stages of evolution must repeat in the newly evolved Being. I must relive my past to evolve into my future. The nearly unbearable ambivalence I felt that first day at Exeter is the same as I now feel about my book. I have been snatched from familiar clutches and I have no choice but to move forward.

THE DRUMBEAT ROLLS WITH FURY

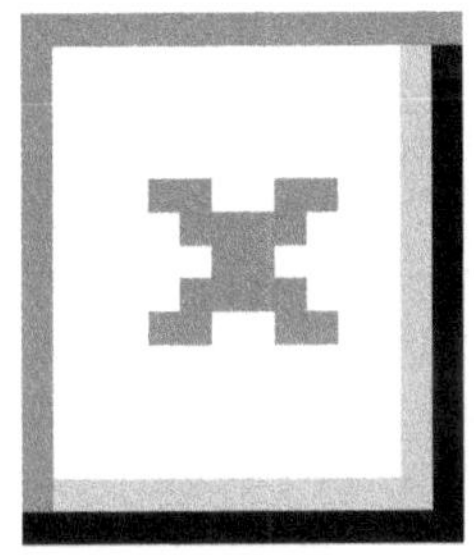

LIGHTNING STRIKES

Zeus is angry. The Bible was tossed at my four-year-old brother's head. Now the atlas of my own oppression is hurled at mine.

As a child, I could not stand the anxiety of wondering, in my sleepless agony, what monster might be hiding inside my closet. I'd get out of bed and turn on the bedroom light. That way all that was familiar and safe was visible to me. Then I'd stand at the closet door trembling. The scariest moment was just before I decided to open the door.

I stood at the doors to each chapter that would reveal my four stages of shame-based identity formation, and I balked at each one: *dissociated... codependent... narcissistic... grieving.* Each was more painful to write than the previous. I re-experienced and relived my personal memories and the unmitigated emotional intensity of each segment.

The Berlin Wall has fallen and the separation of the whole has been resolved!

I gradually became aware of how I was subjected to successive, attempted "identity brandings". The 'Why?' was clear: To cement my identity for life. My slave ancestors were branded as slaves, too. Many different owners branded me and each wanted to claim me as "theirs".

My ancestors are freed!

The rage I'd felt at Exeter and Harvard was so empowering! I was about to claim my entitlement to be a unique individual. Then my rage submitted to defeat— into a feeble, restless alder on my first day at medical school. I was kidnapped by my parents' culminating pressure at the final window of vulnerability for personality fixation. I was ambushed in an all-out struggle that lead me astray from my true calling and into a career I did not want.

My mother and father joined hands in a battle against the education that had inspired my unique destiny, and they stood united in their determination to forge a common destiny of their own choosing. My parents won and my destiny was lost. I relinquished my path at the fork in the road to follow my parent's detour.

My wings were clipped, my anger was tamed, and my individuation was suppressed. I was enrolled in medical school. I was forced to give up my passion for communication, languages, writing and the rarest gift of all: The gift of psychic empathy. I had to conform, be "realistic", and practice medicine like my father.

They will say and they will always believe that I selected my career on my own. It's funny how people's memories can distort whatever may induce shame or guilt. They will rationalize that their reasoning was based on the best available wisdom at the time, about race and opportunity and security. I never try to argue with somebody when they are rationalizing their own reasoning.

Rip van Winkle has finally awakened.

I've had to reclaim that rage to pick up the process of individuation that was curtailed and exiled back into my closet thirty-five years ago. I've always suppressed my rage and I've always been depressed. Without my anger, I could only grieve the loss of something priceless: My true self had been stolen from me.

INDIVIDUATION

*

The angry Gods punish Prometheus for bestowing the gift of fire to empower humans. They bind the immortal to a rock and vultures come every day to eat his liver, which grows back again each night.

As a child, I had to open the door to my bedroom closet. I had to see what was crouching inside the hidden part of my room. I had to know the truth and face it with courage. The moment came when I shifted from fear into anger at the "intruder". I'd take a deep breath and fortify my little muscles and slam the sliding door open, defiantly shouting, "BOO!" — To scare the ghost.

The scariest moment of my life finally arrived yesterday. I stood trembling at the threshold of momentous psychic change. I mustered my rage and threw open the door. Inside, I found my missing soul and my true destiny. They were bound and gagged by old patterns based in shame, anxiety, hatred and grief. I've cut loose the ropes, pulled out the gags, and dispelled the myth of the crouching monster.

De-bugged and de-programmed...

One of the greatest tragedies of social development is the loss of one's identity and mission in life. In our culture, creative freedom is curtailed in the window of the late teenage years up to the early twenties. That's the last chance to "brand" a fixed ethos, along with a career or relationship pattern, on the human brain. The final maturation of the most delicate and significant part of the brain occurs at that time. It is the part that suppresses or promotes one's destiny: *The prefrontal lobes.*

I remember watching an episode of "The Twilight Zone," or perhaps a movie, in which all humans were to be programmed for their specific careers and a guaranteed successful future, and all at the same age— their twenty-first birthday. They would select the career they wanted and then sit in a contraption with a metal cap covering their brains to receive the appropriate imprint. There was no need for education. Then off they would trot, ready to start work.

But sometimes a youth could not be programmed. The protagonist was such an unfortunate; the metal cap didn't work. He pleaded for another chance. Still, failure... His family and friends shunned him. He was a tragic freak that had no place in society. Now he could only await his fate: He would be discarded. He expected to be taken away to somewhere remote, maybe another planet, maybe to death.

43

The men came to cart him away to the special place. He was taken to a secret haven of luxury and intellectual excitement unknown to ordinary people, where all those who *also* had brains resistant to the programming welcomed him with love and respect. A failure to be molded by the cap proved that one had a creative genius! Now he belonged to the transcendent few that were secretly masterminding and inventing the evolving world of the ordinary.

Can we all be de-programmed?

I can "feel" my own brain changing inside my head, even though one cannot feel the brain. I can "see" my brain exposed to my eyes, even though only by symbolism. I now have greater power to re-create my identity, my Self, and all the images, beliefs and behaviors that stream out of it.

*

Prometheus is released from captivity and the gift of fire is restored to all humans.

Only an outsider can point out the obvious. The child who is not caught in the web of collective delusion says that the emperor has no clothes. My writing led to another sort of awareness. I saw the big picture of the heretofore-unwritten synopsis of how shame crystallizes into fixed identity patterns.

I also saw the evil Big Brother of the social implications of shame-based templates that are handed out to the proletariat. The assembly-line models of oppression are branded onto almost all human beings.

I realized that a new global slavery has unmistakably, and ever more cleverly, returned, and that whips and chains are obsolete. It has swept up nearly every human being into a rising tide of shame-based subjugation. It has jammed us into increasingly restricted identities and social roles that fully maintain the status quo.

Has the sea swallowed up Atlantis—is it too late?

*

Many years ago, I began to have nightly experiences, unordinary dreams. Each night, a dove circled over my head as I walked along a windy ocean beach. The dove would drop a feather that fell into my hair and entered my brain. I instantly awoke and "knew" a piece of a puzzle that evolved into an integrated model of psycho-spirituality. This happened every night, exactly at 2am, for six weeks.

Then, one night the dove lingered over my head and shook its wings ferociously. *All* its plumage cascaded as a massive transmission onto and into my head. I awoke feeling near death; my temperature had dropped below normal, I was shaking uncontrollably, vomiting and petrified. I told whatever it was, that I was not ready and I could not cope with the psychic shift. "STOP! GO AWAY!" I shouted. I did not see the bird for several months.

Then it reappeared. I was again walking along a beach and I saw a tree stump embedded in the sand. I approached the oddity. It was just a six-foot tall post with two leafless branches creating a niche for a nest.

Suddenly fierce gales gusted sand in my eyes. The familiar dove arose from the nest and flapped its wings with fury, knocking the nest off the tree stump. In mid-air, a small baby bird was abruptly ousted from its nest and unfurled its virgin wings. It hovered in front of my eyes, looking at me.

I knew that, someday, I would do the same as the baby bird.

This longer segment accurately describes my transcendent experience of releasing major trauma, transforming my neuroanatomy, and experiencing a spiritual epiphany.

SNAP!

It happened on February 24th, 2010. I had an experience of spiritual transcendence. I had planned to have a spiritual and biological transformation because I know what I'm doing to my brain and I know how to change its structure. I've done that for many other people. I'm an expert at tinkering. I forged and labored to make my miracle happen.

I anticipated an evolutionary shift of my Self after working through my impressionable early years and my formative years up until the early twenties. I wanted to make the transformation happen because I'd promised it to the readers and it was an important part of my book. I continued to plan how to force the change in my brain. I had to reconfigure a new brain—*now!*

My adventure of recovery happened as I predicted.

But it was not what I had expected.

During the two anguishing weeks of writing before February 24th, 2010, I unearthed the shame-based roots of my entire life. The process of self-discovery dug to the depths of the mine where I was trapped. But I kept adding more to my to-do list.

I felt escalating pressure to achieve the impossible.

The book had to be an award-winning bestseller, a landmark treatise, and a perfect tome. I had to prepare for success: presentations, media appearances, even being hounded by reporters and carloads of the curious finding out where I live to come and stare at me. I had to prepare for failure: scandals, calamity, publisher's rejections, and my mother's suicide.

I had to overcome all my traumas and be off all my medications. I had to rebuild my entire social life from zero to infinity. I had to get my body into looking like an Adonis, as I'd done before, in an estimated six weeks if I spent three hours a day working out. I had to achieve full individuation from my mother's control and be financially self-sufficient within four months when my disability ran out.

But I was falling behind. I was not making my bed military-style and keeping my apartment spotlessly clean. What would my mother think if she saw the mess? My mother…

I've got to finish the book because it will force her to validate my individuality and make her know me. But what if the book is too much exposure and it will make her hate and disown me instead? I want to *please* her, but she wants me to *be* her. So, I must *rebel* against her. Honor thy parents? Honor thy *children!* Sacrifice my life for them? Live my own life and be true to my Self! I'm torn between pleasing and rebelling.

Time urgency to achieve more and achieve faster soared too high to bear. Icarus was losing his caution and forgetting his father's warning. My expectations reached an apogee of climactic absurdity. The weight of more and more baggage, of overloaded expectations, carried in the passenger basket required more and more helium in the balloon. Suddenly, the explosively compressed balloon mushroomed—**SNAP!**

And the balloon exploded.

When I reviewed the resources that I needed in the original chapter five, I realized that my education had branded all the prerequisite resources needed to heal an anger-based identity—except for relaxation and contentment. Those resources were denied; they might curb the incessant and competitive drive for achievement.

INDIVIDUATION

"The habit of tension is yet with me, but weakens every year that passes…
As I become more and more content and serene."
[From my mother's diary]

My mother was beating her drum of *wanting* contentment, but she never attained it. To rest on her laurels of contentment was postponed and contingent upon the day her sons would meet stringent criteria under her godly countenance.

The transcendent experience that I was about to have was not like my mother's constant rushing to achieve and prepare for the moment when contentment would someday appear. It was not like her "little black book" of tasks and to-dos that had become increasingly chaotic over many decades and generations of little black book after book.

My mother tells me that she is now rushing to purge all her boxes of bric-a-brac and memorabilia and photos, so that everything will be neat and tidy when she dies, or before she develops some crippling brain dysfunction like Alzheimer's. She must be prepared for the wretched fate that she fully anticipates any day now, and which she mentions every time I visit her.

When my mother was about to turn five years old, a new dollhouse store announced its opening day in her hometown of Nashville, Tennessee. Grandmother took her to look at the pretty miniature houses in the display window, and soon my mother was enamored with a beautiful two-story model home of her dreams. There would be enough money to pay for it for her fifth birthday.

A line of eager children and their mothers formed in front of the store on the opening day. The store's owner stood at the doorway to greet the children. When my mother arrived at the door, the owner looked at her skin color and told her that she was not allowed inside.

"GO AWAY! NO COLOREDS ALLOWED!"

Perhaps that was the day my mother began to construct incessant floor plans in her mind. My mother tries to be the Supreme Architect of the world she possesses. Her endless floor plans and furniture arranging and re-arranging have always plagued her. Her designs for an elaborate nuclear fallout shelter kept her morbidly absorbed for years. "How could we all live together in such a small space, underground, for decades, Mom?" I asked her. Even as a child, the thought of dying from radiation poisoning seemed preferable to the alternative.

All objects must be molded and shaped until "just right." The furniture and the walls must change to suit her new plans and designs.

She felt it was her prerogative and her duty to fashion her sons, just as she designed the floor plans as the Supreme Architect of her houses.

When, by sheer force and manipulation, she gets what she wanted, she looks at the result with critical eyes and decides it's not exactly what she had expected. The plans reverse, the course veers left and right and around in circles. The truth is that what she had truly expected was not a rearrangement of existing pieces in the external and material world of things and objects, including people. *The problem is that she had expected to feel the state of contentment itself.* The perfect arrangement of the furniture and the perfect compliance of her sons to her predetermined designs cannot produce contentment.

The problem is also that she never changed the house of her own mind. Someday, she might come to "like" the house of her Self, of her sons, of her residence. My mother's wish that she and her sons have a contented life represents an end-point state of existence. Perhaps, she meant that we might experience contentment in the *process* of living?

Suddenly I don't care about the philosophical or psychological details. Is it possible to just be contented without any need to do or achieve anything or to prove myself to anybody?

I felt escalating pressure to know the unknowable.

The more I tried to "design" my future, the more unknowable it became. I have never experienced such uncertainty about my book, and about my future relationships, lifestyle, career, or finances. Anything and everything may soon change. The unknown is scary and my old ego doesn't like the unknown. If I thought about my future, I could not focus on the writing.

I discovered that the only way to proceed with my writing was to shift into a meditative state of mind, and to live in The Zone of each tiny moment of the creative process without regard to future outcomes. The rigorous process of writing forced me to focus on smaller and smaller bits of time.

As a novice writer, I discovered that what I think I will write is not exactly how it turns out. The finished pieces transcend my plans and fit into the book like cells genetically predetermined to form complex tissues, and into a sequence with a deeper meaning than I had known before writing. I had to be passive and patient. I had to relax and enjoy the natural course of events. I had to surrender to the creative process of life unfolding: "When the words are ready, the writer will come."

I had begun to feel like a lame-duck president making a glowing State of the Union Address about how well he'd performed as president, but the public wasn't interested in listening to the same old lines. Then, I proceeded to feeling that a ghostwriter had written the lines to my speech; they were not my words. I was becoming a fraud, an imposter.

Like my mother, I was forcing the external world to bend to my will on levels where will is not welcome. I was a hypocrite, a demagogue, in a last-ditch hyped-up effort, beating battle drums for war. But the soldiers refused to march. I had been trying to engineer my future. The future is not mine to engineer.

I looked at my notes and plans for the previous day as if a madman had written them: "I am already afraid I've lost the power and the momentum of the book. I must pour all my best material into the next chapter, leaving space for my adventures in the last two chapters. I've got to plan and prepare for chapter six onwards. Maybe, pound with the theme of death? I must force the adventure part and get some extraordinary synchronistic experiences."

But as I proofread the lengthy original chapters, pouring over them in minute detail, I felt like I was slowly becoming a *new* president preparing to move into the Oval Office. Without realizing it, my writing and proofreading were repeatedly triggering, stimulating, and strengthening the neurobiological imprints of my new Self. Doors to my subconscious were flung open by freed memories that emerged from their captivity in the caved-in mine. I began to see that I was proofreading my own brain's circuitry. I didn't have to struggle with locks and chains; they just began to snap open. The miraculous adventure, the creation of the extraordinary, was happening all along.

Then stranger things began to happen…

I began to shift involuntarily into a meditative state of complete calmness without any intention to meditate. The phenomenon was so pleasurable that I soon chose to enter the state and just "sit there." Alarmed a bit by this new development, I tried harder to focus on the proofreading.

Phone-calls…

My brother called me unexpectedly. I told him about the book's progress and read him a little piece. I expected him to stubbornly dismiss my project, but he was intensely interested. I said, "Well, maybe now you can respect me a little bit?"

He replied, "I already *do* respect you, Michael!" He had never said that before—**SNAP!**

My mother's call…

Her fury had resurfaced in narcissistic rage as she cast her murderous death wish upon me. I was not doing her will by writing this book. She knows that I am slipping away into this mysterious book. I am slipping out of her control and that incites her. She is slipping away into her last stage of life, her last chance to make a permanent impression on me that will finally make her feel contented. When I reacted in reciprocal fury, a door opened—**SNAP!**

Gestures…

The next day, I told Christine, my therapist, about my mother's call. She lifted her hand and moved her curled fingers in a rapid guitar-playing gesture to signify "manipulating my mind." What I saw in her gesture was a spider, scurrying along its web. I have a phobia about spiders. Then, I saw my mother as the spider and I was terrified. I have a phobia about my mother.

My therapist asked me, "What happens if you just cut the strings?" I play-acted being a marionette, bouncing about awkwardly on strings tugged by my parents, whose heads were above me, looking down on me, always looking down on me, making me dance. Then, I made a gesture of cutting the strings. I pretended to fall in an exhausted heap on the puppet stage, on my therapist's sofa, free and happy, but not knowing how to move my Self by myself.

Laughter…

Suddenly, I started laughing harder than in my whole life! I laughed with Christine until my belly ached and tears poured out of my eyes. Then I looked at Christine through a new set of eyes, and, in that instant, I loved her. I let *her* consciousness holographically enter *my* mind. In the shared laughter, then a calm surrender, I internalized her as my first unique and loving entity outside of my dysfunctional family. I saw that she was "*not*-mother." She was on my side. *She was inside—* **SNAP!**

The miraculous transformation that happened on February 24th, 2010 was not what I'd expected. The creative process did not lead to an evolutionary shift—a *transcendent* shift happened instead. Although I cannot pinpoint the moment of the breakthrough, nor retrace exactly how it happened, I know that at some point that morning a final **SNAP!** transpired and I transformed.

INDIVIDUATION

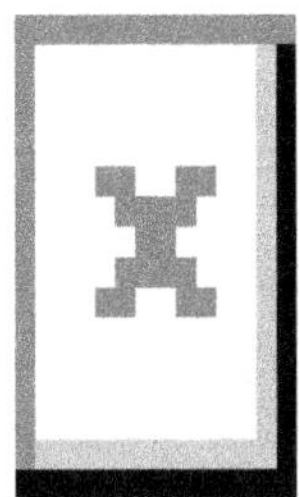

Light bulbs…

It was the day after I saw the spider in my therapist's hand gesture. I was sitting on my bed proofreading the piece about when my mother attacked me, scratching at my face. I heard a crash of breaking glass and I assumed it came from outdoors. I went into my study to retype the piece and saw that the light bulb of my desk lamp had somehow ejected itself onto my desk and broken into shards of glass all over my manuscript and notes. I glanced at the piles of notes that seemed to reach the ceiling. I began to clean up the mess and vacuum the glass. I took the broken fragments of my light bulb into the kitchen to toss them into my large trashcan. I turned on the overhead stove-hood light. It came on, and then—FLASH! It exploded internally and blew out.

SNAP! —SNAP!! —SNAP!!!

A bright light turned on inside me, together with a voice that said: "You don't have to be afraid anymore, Michael." I kept hearing and saying the words as if each time were the first time.

*

Time stops and I stop as I enter the present, the now. My body transports me to my bed and I sit here for a long time. I draw a picture of radiation from beyond passing through a smiling sun onto me. Beams of energy break through the clouds in which my head floats.

The picture shows me walking on the ocean of my subconscious. I write: "Air. Force only air."

All my senses become hypersensitive. I feel the cool temperature of my bedroom and the minutest breeze on my skin. I see a tiny ant moving in the remote distance and watch it through the finder of my eyes. My lips are dry. I open my chapstick and feel and smell the lubricant spreading on my lips. I re-cap the chapstick and hear a booming "click." My sensory brain is changing.

My emotions are shifting every few minutes. I feel anxiety that alternates with calmness as vast as the universe, as if I were floating in a sensory isolation tank. I close my eyes into eternity and I know that the death of my old Ego is happening. I start to cry, then I laugh, then I am angry—without any images or thoughts to provoke the feelings. My emotional mid-brain is changing.

A cross-circuiting process is happening as my memories become clear with the speed of a stroke. Compulsive shame-based patterns are dissolving, or disengaging with the sensation of gears pulling separate from other gears and still revolving, but not connecting. They are just wheels in motion. Memory centers of my cerebral cortex are changing.

Images begin to appear. I am rescued from the mineshaft and resurface to enjoy the fresh air in a garden above. I see that my boat, the book, has capsized. It's OK if my boat sinks, because I know I can swim the whole lap now.

There are strong arms that lift me up from beyond. Or perhaps it feels that I can fly up, transcend upwards as if in a bubble of the "Good Witch of the North," and see myself in a faraway future with visionary precognition. Or, just by clicking my heels, I can "know" my destiny without seeing its face close-up. My occipital and temporal cortices are changing.

My identity is reconfigured. I split into four simultaneous lives, tracing time from now to the eternal beyond. Each of my Selves is complete and contented, enjoying their endless moment. As I blend into them, each subpersonality links me to current life experiences. I can clearly envision myself in my own future! My frontal lobes are changing.

My shame-based, dissociated part—from birth to age seven—chooses to stay on the restful island. Bountiful food becomes available and he plans to explore the whole island and build a home like Robinson Crusoe, where he would be a homebody and a nobody and relax. He has nothing to say. Without having to feel like he was a bad boy in an unsafe world, he **SNAPS** out of his shame!

INDIVIDUATION

My fear-based part, age seven to fourteen, gets in the rowboat and picks up the oars. Then, he starts rowing across the calm strait toward the sunny Silver City, but he no longer feels any compulsion to arrive there. In fact, he doesn't even look at the silver dot on the horizon. He is happy with the simple process of rowing across the sea. It has become a magnificent and delightful movement that he deeply enjoys.

As I blend into him in the humble boat, my parental insistence on "moral perfection" and my academic brandings to "achieve, always achieve" both evaporate into thin air, *gone away*.

My fear-based part tells me: "You don't have to achieve a state of not having to achieve, anymore." He explains that I have given him so much to do, such impossible-to-achieve expectations, that he simply gives up. He relinquishes the burden of trying to please authority figures or get validation from a peer group anymore. Without having to please those who abuse him, he simply **SNAPS** out of his anxiety!

My anger-based part, age fourteen to twenty-one, still has some work to do; the last tough root of my shame is still embedded like a festering ingrown toenail. Surgery is required to achieve my independence. My parents stand in the way, boasting of their righteous worry and prayers, and inserting hopelessness and shame about my unsalvageable salvation.

The repressed rage of my squelched adolescent rebellion twists my focus onto my parents by strobe light, then by laser. I merge into their minds again, to see myself through their massively distorted eyes, and I do not like what I see. But I must see it. I must know their Truth. Then, I smash the funhouse mirror of their unreal image of me that has warped my soul and my life. I smash the mirror like the rocks hurled by racist Klansmen who could not see the real "us" once left a carpet covered with broken glass upon which my father slept with a shotgun for a week.

My anger-based part tells me: "The time has come to let go of your parents! Their power must be nullified and their engulfment repelled. They have usurped your dignity and distorted your self-concept for long enough. As of this moment, you are already a unique and independent individual and a great man by all who choose to really know you!"

Then he transports to the Silver City where he already is, right now, in a simultaneous life. He is giving lectures and talks about shame to very interested audiences. Contented and confident that my boundaries are now tough enough to guard against my parents' manipulations, he **SNAPS** out of his hatred!

My grieving part, starting at age twenty-one, lets go of this world and transcends into a conscious concurrent afterlife, from which he watches over the other three parts of me. He watches over the total "me," joyously contemplating the meaning of my whole life's process up until my death. He also appears to be birthing my new Self, perhaps to be known as my Fifth Self, perhaps as my love-based subpersonality, or perhaps simply, my soul. My grieving part tells me: "Your vision is now rooted in Faith. I promise you shall have a positive and meaningful future." Re-accessing a sense of optimistic realism, he easily **SNAPS** out of his grief!

An image then forms of my new love-based part. I hover now even higher, above the grieving Self, and see my lineage of slave ancestors whose bodies belonged to their master, and all of whom were forced to achieve until death came from overwork. *"Plant the crops! Harvest the cotton! All hands including children must work from dawn to dusk!"*

Even more, I see the mixed-race house slaves who were enmeshed and more emotionally wounded than by the physical scars of whips, burnings, mutilations and beatings in the field. I feel waves of compassion for my mother, as a wounded child whose offers of love I've come to distrust, fearing the strings that are always attached. I hover above the lineage of all my exes. I see my ex-partners as traumatized children who did the same as my mother.

Through this new love-based identity, I have attained an ability to just close my eyes and drift into a state of relaxation and contentment and faith and individuation all together—to just STOP and enjoy the magical process of my life's unfolding.

When I first embarked upon this writing journey two months ago, an epiphany occurred as I saw a way out of my suffering and a creative process was engendered. Now, it seems that transcendence has begun to manifest as love-based imprints replace shame-based ones.

My old ego whimpers: "How extraordinarily ordinary!" To be contented in the moment and have faith in the unknown future is nothing to boast about. The adventure is not about forging external changes and making miracles happen; it's about allowing myself to be fully human and to like the house I live in—if I can live in my house and not be a house slave in another's!

Having experienced contentment and faith to the degree I did on February 24th, 2010, I can often go back to the same, perfect, meditative state just by closing my eyes. The process of my life's mission rises from a foundation of contentment. The state of my life's vision is built on the bedrock of faith. Both are now as solid as was the Holy Mount of Jerusalem.

I will manifest the last set of my missing resources by finding healthy, loving peers. My dissociated child Self will have playmates, not just sex-mates. My self-sacrificing codependent Self will have friendships, peers, and an intimate partner, not narcissistic predators. My tough, angry adolescent Self will have a public audience, not sparring critics. My tragic, sad, and grieving Self will unite with co-visionaries, not just patients and clients.

And what about my transcendent and love-based Self? He will know soulmates; although that's the stuff of which heaven is made. On Earth, they appear by accident and synchronicity. It's just a matter of recognizing them when they arrive.

Together, all my Selves embody a message in a bottle from beyond:
"KEEP SWIMMING!"
"KEEP RUNNING!"
"KEEP DANCING!"
"KEEP ROWING!"
"KEEP ENJOYING!"
"KEEP YOUR FAITH!"
"KEEP ON YOUR PATH!"
"Don't let others lead you astray, Michael."

*

My days since February 24th have been emotionally unpredictable. Like the early springtime weather outside, rainstorms alternate with sunshine in quick flashing cycles. The psychic change seems to be simmering and this is a supremely delicate time with shaky progress. My emotional brain is still catching up with the flash re-patterning of my cerebral cortex. Twenty-one years of developmental programming and trauma have dissipated, leaving only one last ghost in my closet.

I know that the deep brain trauma patterns are now disrupted and a sequence of new patterns will take a while to fully mature and get established. I will rest and sleep, as my brain and my body demand it. A command on my computer screen usually appears when I've downloaded a new program: "Restart your computer." I see the parallel to my brain, but the turning-off to allow the new patterns to integrate into my anatomy takes a long time to congeal.

Deep, divine sleep…then, I'll be ready to pass between the eyes of the flanking Matriarchal Sphinxes without fear. The last battle of my war for independence will now begin. I must vanquish the core root of my interpersonal shame and the full history of my toxic *adult* relationships.

GIFTS FROM A GODDESS

Athena appeared in a dream, as she had to Odysseus in his times of tribulation.
She brought gifts that I will need on the journey for the rest of my life:
A *blueprint* of my shame-based patterns is in my hands—
My neural imprints, etchings, brandings, scripts, traces, signatures, engrams…
A *map* and a *compass* are given to me!
I have faith that I can steer clear of the rocks in the sea of oppression.
I know the safest passage to the Silver City ahead, but it is not a direct, easy route.
I have been given the *sword* to cut through my illusion of unworthiness,
Hermes' *winged shoes* to transcend to the skies of contentment,
A *magic lute* to put the Cyclops of Narcissism to sleep,
And *conch shells* to mask the Sirens of my internal doubts.
I have been given a *magnifying glass*, through which I can focus light like a prism onto shame,
And burn through it like paper.
And, the most valuable of all her gifts, is a *magic mirror!*
It reveals in stark exposure the naked truth of my loving individuality.
It can show the narcissist, Medusa, her hair of coiled vipers and she will let me go.

THE STRONG STEADY DRUMBEATS BEGIN AGAIN

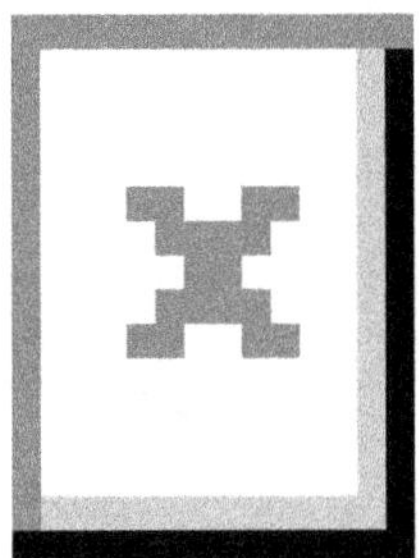

This is a vital and epitomized depiction of my mother's mental illness and child abuse. It contains shocking memories of her most damaging and traumatizing behavior, with a psychological and metaphysical angle. The ending is compassionate and forgiving.

THE LAST SLAP OF THE PAPER DRAGON'S TAIL

March 10, 2010

The past four days have been a struggle with my Shadow in the cave—she didn't want me to leave her and she wanted to stay in her underworld confinement.

Years ago, when I was at the nadir of depression and alcoholism, I visualized descending into my Underworld cave to find the image behind my drinking. I expected to find an image depicting my troubled Self in the cave. Instead, I discovered my mother, crouched and huddled over the perennial razor blade, her hair falling over her tear-streaked face, just as I'd often found her at home.

Yesterday, I saw the same image. I tried to console her and show her that there was sunshine up above. I pointed to the speck of light visible at the distant entrance to the subterranean cavern. I tugged on her arm to entice her to get up and walk out, but she would not budge. She was deeply entranced, contemplating the blade, mumbling to the blade and to her morbid self.

What self-destructive identity was she doomed to endure? Now I understand how Mom was programmed to be a facsimile of her own subconsciously hated father, and would therefore attack aspects of her own Self that were introjected from him. Her depression and suicide attempts were perhaps aborted efforts to kill Herbert Milo Holloway, her father within her own psyche and soul.

I have wrenched sharp objects away from her, before they cut her or me. Yet so close they would come. I had to survive and somehow I managed to do what I had to do, always just in time. I don't know how I had the timing and the strength as a child. I have only a few scars outside, but so many inside me.

The needle that pierced her sinful hand twenty times for the twenty questions on the French exam, the razor blades hovering over her wrists, the knives and scissors that pointed at herself and at my childhood neck—until I'd panic whenever somebody held a knife, just for food preparation or for any innocent reason for the rest of my life.

Why did she hate me as the projection of herself so much?

The paradoxes are clearer now: I am given the best education, but noticeable achievement is discouraged to prevent a replay of her tragic life as a prodigy. I must behave like a saint, but fit in as ordinary. Any deviation from her childhood obedient house slave identity is evil and my mother is compelled to try to destroy it. Any adolescent instinct I have smirks of King Kong grandfather and the rebellious field slave identity. It, too, must be murdered to convert her son to being a safe and docile replica of herself as a little girl.

Christine, my therapist, helped me realize yesterday that I could not save my mother. She loved Thanatos, the death wish, and the Underworld more than she loved me. It's like the myth of Orpheus who cannot bring his beloved Eurydice back to life from Hades…

"But now they were almost there, the blackness was turning gray.
Now Orpheus had stepped out joyfully into the daylight.
Then he turned to see Eurydice.
It was too soon; she was still in the cavern.

INDIVIDUATION

He saw her in the dim light, and he held out his arms to clasp her; but
on the instant, she was gone.
She had slipped back into the darkness."
"All Orpheus heard was one faint word, 'Farewell.'"

In the imagery, I told her, "I've done all I can for you, Mom, and
I've failed. You're on your own now." It is true that I've done all I
could to please and protect my mother. I, we, have tiptoed around
Mom our entire lives, in dread of her ultimate threat: the weapon of
self-destruction. My mother has often declared, "If I really did what
you say I did to you, Michael, then I could not bear to live with
myself."

I, we, have lied and kept secrets to protect her. My father, who
witnessed much of what happened, will become furious if I talk about
the domestic violence. He has sworn to protect Mom's right for denial
and denounces me as a liar. I would desist, suppressing the truth yet
once again. I don't like being called a liar or a child who exaggerates

and makes up stories at age fifty-five. I've conspired in building a fallout shelter of distortion around my mother for her safety.

I forgive my mother for everything, including her repressed memories. My father did not know that barbiturates cause loss of both inhibition and memory. I will someday celebrate a Christmas without hearing Mom wailing in hysteria and frightening us all. All those Christmases, every joyless holiday of my youth, that was filled with torment…

My mother handed me two gifts on my tenth birthday: the beautiful, illustrated book I'd wanted a long time, "Gulliver's Travels," and a kit to make giant soap bubbles. I remember how nervous I was when she handed me the gifts; I sensed she was on edge. So, I thanked her and took them to my bedroom. I closed the door quietly. I placed the presents on my dresser and sat on my bed looking at them with joyful contentment. I didn't even want to open the book because it was too precious to touch.

I did not protest and I did not cry when my mother threw the door open, screaming, "YOU'RE UNGRATEFUL!" She opened the bottle of soap solution and poured it onto the beautiful pages of the book in front of my face, making sure to soak every chapter. Then, she threw the book at me with curses and poured the rest of the soap over my body. I have never read "Gulliver's Travels." I just can't bear to read it, but I imagined that I'd already read it. When the door slammed shut and the tears came, I was in the land of the Lilliputians, bound and tied by their strings to the ground.

I studied piano, hoping to please my mother. She fired my piano teacher because she wasn't strict enough. My mother could hear the minutest mistake, even when she was in a room far away and behind several closed doors. She listened to my music, even though I played so quietly, so pianissimo. I felt terror with each note and chord, praying it would be correct and trying to practice without her hearing me.

"B-FLAT, MICHAEL! Why can't you get it right! What's the matter with you?" she shrieks from beyond. She could hear my error no matter how silently I played. Then she would appear at the piano, incensed and threatening that if I continued to upset her like this….

I gave up my practice one day when my mother sat beside me on the bench. She couldn't stand to hear my wrong note the third time and slammed the keyboard cover down on my fingers, trying to break them all. But I read her mind and had a split second to save my hands.

When I was sixteen, just before I had a driver's license, my mother came to pick me up from my one and only date with a beautiful black girl, Vicki Taylor. Vicki was giving me the first French kiss of my life; she wrapped her leg around mine and I lost myself into her embrace. It was a moment of unforgettable intimacy, of pure delight, standing on the sidewalk in Erie that warm spring night.

But my mother's car turned the corner just at that moment. In tragic anticipation, I endured a twenty-minute ride home in total silence, during which I could not move or look at my mother. I felt her envious scorn. When we got home, my mother could not contain her jealousy.

She ripped and tore off all her clothes, screaming, **"FUCK ME, LIKE YOU WANT TO FUCK THAT BITCH!"** She chased me naked through the house, cornering me, shoving me against walls, armed with a butcher's knife, gesturing at her vagina and then, with murderous intent, my neck.

"Grandpa saw my mother receive a sweet good-bye kiss from the boy…his draconian punishment was to refuse to say a single word to his daughter for two entire years. It was during those years that Mom began to experience depression."

I asked my mother to help type a hundred-page paper on my studies of thirteen groups engaged in altered states of consciousness that were active in Boston in 1972. I was passionately excited about neuropsychology after coming back from Haiti. I had incredible findings to document and I expressed my excitement to my grim-faced mother. Haiti had inspired the paper, which marked the turning point of my spiritual awakening and the birth of my life's mission. My mother stood in the hallway holding the pages in her hands, staring at me, rolling her eyes, switching her hips, making insulting gestures and mocking faces at me.

Then she snarled, "You think you know everything, don't you, MR. KNOW-IT-ALL!" She threw the pile of un-typed pages into the air and at me. She would never, ever, encourage, praise, or validate my achievements. That could make me feel proud of myself or allow me to be a separate individual.

I, we, walked on eggshells around Mom, honoring the total silence of her depressed tomb. Everything I've done, all the decisions I've ever made, always carried the questions: *What would my mother want me to do? Will I have to add it to the pile of secrets? How will this affect my mother? Will it please her?*

It seemed that I could never please my mother. Her double binds were so erratic that to do one thing, to do the opposite thing, to do a compromised middle thing—everything was wrong. I, we, have let

Mom live in her conscious world of self-righteous condescension. I have tolerated her not seeing the relationship between her sons' troubles in later adult life and our mixed signals, abuse, and the disturbed bonding with her disturbed soul.

I came very close to giving up writing this book to please my mother these past four days since the last phone call. I must not do anything that could make me feel proud. I labored in horrible inertia and my transcendent experience sank under her curse upon my endeavor. The dragon roared and lunged up from the cave to engulf me in fire and threaten my survival.

To write about solipsism and engulfment is to write about the greatest human abuse possible. It is to throw oneself upon the funeral pyre to join the deceased husband. It is having a gun held to one's head and being ordered to dig your own grave. It is to be mummified and buried alive deep inside the pyramid's crypt with the Pharaoh, my Master. It is the equivalent of being forced to carry one's cross and nailing one's self to it. I have nailed myself to my cross, next to the cross my mother is on. I can hear her wailing engrained in my mind. Since before I can remember, I can hear it anytime. She has languished her entire lifetime, moaning, bemoaning, and preparing to die.

'Mom, I've done all I can for you, and I've failed to make you happy. It's all up to you now. I know you really love me.'

'Dad, I must let go of trying to please you, too. I know your Truth and it doesn't matter anymore. What matters is that I know you really love me.'

And I will finish this book. I will be free. I know the paper dragon's tail will try to slap me again because that's its nature and I'm OK with it.

"SNAP!"

"SNAP!"

"SNAP!"

Something strange is happening again. I just finished proofreading this segment and went outside to my patio. The sounds of traffic on the highway and the wind were gone. Instead, I heard soft, peaceful, beautiful piano music. It came from "nowhere." After a long while, the piano music that I used to play faded.

THE DRUMBEATS RESUME IN SONOROUS TEMPO

SEQUENCE FOUR: CAREER IDENTITY

The common experience of derailing a youngster's true choice of career and imposing a "mind cap" of a completely incongruent nature is one of society's most devastating events. It occurs typically in the early 20's and represents a re-structuring of the prefrontal lobes of the brain—as I discuss in my book, "Overcoming Oppression."

CAREER IDENTITY FORECLOSURE

I am sitting in the farthest back corner of "Amphitheater C" at Harvard Medical School, reading Italian short stories and practicing invisibility. Just as I once pretended to "sleep like an angel" with my blankets over my head, I must now seclude myself from my classmates.

It's "hide and play dead" all over again. And it's the first day of a career that will last thirty-five years. I'd just flown back from Europe the night before and this place seems surrealistic and unreal. 'It's just another city. It's a very strange city. I'll travel on soon.' I hear myself thinking and *wishing* it were true.

But I can't pretend. I realize that a brutal indoctrination has begun. The most heinous of all possible professional etchings awaits me. Grief and depression has set in and will last a very long time. How did I get here? I've been hijacked off my route. I retrace the events that led to an ill-fated turn at a fork in the road of my destiny.

Exeter—all the honors and prizes pointed to a career in diplomacy and international affairs. I was offered a scholarship to study in France my senior year, but my parents refused to allow it. "How will you take *science* courses in France?" my father asks.

"NO, Dad. I don't *want* to take more science courses. I want to study languages and foreign cultures!" I protest vehemently. My father is huddling with my mother on their strategy before the kick-off. I have a strong offense but a weak defense, and he's going to get the ball.

I remind them about my prowess and love of learning languages. "Any darn foreigner can speak their own language *and* English better than you'll ever be able to! Why on Earth do you want to major in romance languages and literature? It's a waste of your time. Major in a science!"

"*NO*, Dad. Why do you keep prodding me to go to medical school?" I kick off the football. My father grabs it and makes a good run to the 100-yard line.

I tell them about my discoveries in psychology and human consciousness. But they don't listen to me or they poke fun at it. I tell Dad about my international friends…

My father would lie, if he thought the lie would work to achieve his ends. One of his favorite techniques was saying he'd hired a private detective to prove I was wrong about somebody like Jaimes. Then I'd tell him about my adventures or my memories of the past, and he would accuse me of making it all up.

Dad always laughs at me for being foolish and tells me to be *realistic* every time I talk to him. "You just have to *realize* that…." I'd finish the sentence in my mind: "The only real world is *my* world and your world is *unreal.*"

"Michael! You're being naïve and foolish again. You're thinking like a six-year-old. You must be realistic!" He adds, "I've done well as a doctor, and blacks can't do *better* than that! Will you just take the pre-med course curriculum? *PLEASE?* We're paying for your education and it's creating financial hardships for us. You owe it to us. So, take a few courses, just to see how well you do."

"*NO*, Dad. Why do you keep pushing me to go to medical school?" My father is at the 50-yard line.

My white freshman advisor concurs, "*No* black has a chance in diplomacy! Even African nations would consider a black ambassador second-rate!" Later, I will realize how mistaken my advisor was: Andrew Young? Barak Obama? *Inconceivable…*

"OK. Since you're paying for college, I'll compromise. I'll have *three* majors. I'll double major in psychology and social relations *and* in romance languages and literature, *and* I'll take the pre-med courses. But remember, I said, *NO*. I don't want to go to medical school."

"Michael! You're so *smart!* You've gotten all those A's in the science courses. You even got the top grade above everybody in the most difficult pre-med course, organic chemistry. It would be a shame to waste such good grades. You must apply to medical schools, just to see if you get in."

"*NO, DAD!* I don't *want* to go to medical school!" My father is at the 5-yard line and pushing for the goal.

INDIVIDUATION

'Michael! We're so immensely pleased! You got accepted to all the top medical schools! Harvard, Princeton, Yale, Stanford…now, which one would you *like* to go to?" my father exhorts.

'*GOAL!*'

Thirty years later, my father will apologize for pushing me into his footsteps as a doctor. He will admit that the field of medicine changed in the hands of profiteers that will strip the doctor of privileges and mandate abominable working conditions. But he will never admit that I was abducted from my true passion and innate gifts. I will point out to my father that the profession is now bankrupt of the *art* of healing and the *ethics* of basic honesty.

He will reply, "You just have to *realize*, Michael, that's the way it is. You'll have to swallow your pride and do whatever they tell you to do, even if it's dishonest and fraudulent. You've got to make money or you won't survive."

Finally, he will say to me, "Besides, you're too *old* to change now!"

*

I look around at my ninety-nine classmates. The stats: 1975 and the all-time peak of medical school applications, with *twenty thousand* eager students vying for any *one* available position at Harvard, and all were qualified. Half of my graduating class at Harvard was pre-med; ten percent got to enter here today. That means that fifty out of the hundred students here in Amphitheater C are people I should recognize. I see them in the packed front rows and thankfully most of them are far away from me. They are the students who I'd scrupulously avoided for the past four years in college.

About twenty percent of the class, those in the front rows who arrive early, is the group of dissociated, nerdish fact-gatherers. *They forage for data like berries and roots.* They are all wearing white dress shirts with a neat array of pencils and pens in the left shirt pocket. They will pursue a future in medical research.

About sixty percent are the arch-competitive narcissists. *They are the carnivorous hunters.* They expect money and power, as well as the best seats in the amphitheater, even when they arrive late. They will become the most highly paid super-specialists.

The final twenty percent is in the middle to the rear. They politely saved empty seats in front of them for those who might arrive late. *They are the squaws of the tribe who cook and clean the cave or tent.* They are the token evidence of Harvard's limited concession to the early 70's tide of reformist social conscience. They are the anxious and self-sacrificing caregivers who will experience chronic burnout as clinicians in major inner-city hospitals. They will serve the poor and needy.

I glance at some of the new students and the usual medley of dignitaries is present. There is Richard G. Rockefeller. He has flown his private plane here to join us. I will soon see him hovering over a microscope and wannabes hovering over him. He's actually a nice fellow, one of the *not* shame-based people, and endowed with modesty and empathy as well as money. He will become a philanthropist and disburse many tens or hundreds of millions from his family's charitable foundations for medical research.

I wonder if he knows that his ancestor's billions "bought" the medical field in the 1910s. John D. Rockefeller and Andrew Carnegie disfigured the art of compassionate healing into their vision of a world based on science and mechanistic industry. Soon, *Great Gatsby* prototypes of "Gentlemen Doctors" were designed and rolled off the assembly line to produce an elite caste that excluded women, blacks, and the poor.

There is Mark Vonnegut, son of the famous writer. He's just written his own bestseller about how he survived a psychotic break. He has not yet learned to control his psychic empathy. He will live an anxious, codependent life until he fortifies his boundaries. I will soon watch him in gross anatomy, shoveling out buckets of fat from an obese cadaver's belly, with his eyes glazed over and…*on the edge?*

Then, there is Scarlet, the unabashed *social predator*. She flaunts both her self-made millions and her body, and tosses her fur coat on the floor like a rag to warm her feet in the front row. She will bluntly tell anybody who asks—and anybody who *doesn't* ask—that she's just here to get leads to more millions. Healing has nothing to do with the petty title to be earned at the end of four years. The MD degree is just a ticket to *very* big bucks.

Scarlet complains about having to learn about Sickle Cell Anemia, which is a grave illness that afflicts African Americans. "Well, what a waste of my time. I'll never have to treat *those* kinds of people!" Years later, in a class reunion report, she will boast about successfully birthing twins after age sixty. She will write that the only thing she would wish to teach her girls is "how to marry into money," so that they won't have to be self-made millionaires, and so they can continue the fabulously wealthy lifestyle that she has had.

INDIVIDUATION

Henceforth, I will *always* sit in the last row, back on the far left of Amphitheater C. As I isolate myself in my private corner, I wonder if this is where my great-uncle Holloway, my grandfather's only full brother, had also sat fifty years earlier—cordoned off with a metallic screen of racial discrimination "for mutual protection."

On paper, I am now a member of the most elite "Guild of Gentleman Physicians." Rote memory replaces creativity and empathy; nurturance and intuition are banished under the registered trademark of research-based medicine. For most of my classmates, love has no value, as they become androids that will be completely programmed to their specific reductionist functions.

I have breached my integrity and I'm trapped in a career that is the antithesis of my soul. Inside, I stifle a tortured voice that screams, 'I don't *want* to be here! I don't *belong* here! I want *OUT* of here!' My subconscious is powerful. It has the power to attract the fate of expulsion by group members if I don't honor its needs.

Saturday mornings, illustrious doctors will present "Grand Rounds" where patients are brought into the amphitheater for questions. I will raise my hand and ask a beautiful young female patient who has just had a colostomy how she feels about the surgery and how it's affected her life…Only to be laughed at and booed by my peers for the stupidity of asking about somebody's feelings. I will see Herbert Benson, MD give his first lectures on the "Relaxation Response," his cornerstone contribution to reviving the heart of medicine. He will also be scoffed and ignored by my new peers.

I will try to find love and acceptance among my classmates, and I will inexorably fail. I will almost always fail to find doctors with their heart and art intact after the "mind cap" of indoctrination has been placed on their skulls. I will announce the formation of a Bisexual-Gay-Lesbian support group to which nobody will dare come. Marvin will slip me a note: 'If I come, I'll have to admit that I'm gay. If I'm gay, then I'll have to see a psychiatrist. If I have to see a psychiatrist, I won't have enough time to study. I'm sorry.'

I hate the cage and the raft and the fork of destiny onto which I've been dragged! I will try to *conform*. But it will drain me. Sooner or later, I will risk all material security as a *non*-conformist, especially when moral and ethical integrity are at stake and patients are being abused. I will try to *compensate*. I will divert my energy to outside adventures and relationships, to redeem the loss of congruence with my career. But then, I will live only half a life. I will try to *compromise*. I will search for a special clause to the general rules; one that allows me to eke out an existence in medicine, infused with my unique "style." But then, I will also fail because compromise with the beast is not allowed, and to compromise is not my Truth.

The beast of self-sabotage is welling up inside me. It feeds on hatred. I must motivate myself by hate, and hate to motivate myself, because that's the nature of the indoctrination that has now begun. This day, the first day of my medical career, I suddenly stop looking in strangers' eyes. If someone looks at me, I avert my gaze. I don't want to let anybody know me…. They might find the BEAST inside of me.

I return to reading my anthology of Italian short stories.

Here is a couplet of brief glimpses at the arrogance and callousness of medical education at Harvard Medical School. The first of the couplet is somewhat humorous, the second quite sad and tear provoking.

THE CHAIRMAN

I recoiled from the elitism of Harvard Medical School, and I spent my years there distracted by relationships, hobbies, and excitement whenever I could. But sometimes, I just had to cry. *Status* far outweighed education in all aspects. There are many stories that I could relate about the top professional school in the period of 1975 to 1980. But I've chosen just a few glimpses of "the stamp of status."

Saturday mornings at Harvard Medical School are dedicated to Grand Rounds for first-year medical students. That's when an illustrious professor presents a case history and then summons the patient into the amphitheater, to be seen and answer questions from the students.

One day, the chairman of the neurology department presents the case of a rare neuromuscular disorder. The hundred students are attentive, as always. Then, the chairman deviates from the usual didactic pattern. He lectures the students on the most important lesson of today's presentation.

"The physician's authority must be automatic and dramatic. The patient must accept his lower status with docility. This is presumed in the doctor-patient relationship, and is vital to the treatment process." He then points to two chairs on the stage: There is a large, padded, leather wingchair that he names "The Harvard Chair." Next to it is a smaller, straight-backed wooden chair without arms.

The chairman continues, "When the doors open and the patient enters, you will notice that the patient's natural response will be to sit in the *meeker* chair, and leave the *better* chair for me!"

The doors open and a thin, nervous man peeks in at the assemblage of Harvard students. Then he staggers into the amphitheater, limping and twitching from his condition. He notices the two chairs. He chooses the nicer chair.

I initiate an enthusiastic round of applause, but only a few of my classmates join me. The chairman of the neurology department at Harvard Medical School looks aghast. He orders a stagehand to bring him *another* "Harvard Chair."

He is the "Chair Man," after all.

*

THE DONUT MAN

It's surgical Grand Rounds at the Robert Bent Brigham Hospital—the premier surgical teaching hospital in the nation and perhaps in the world in 1978. An entourage of about twenty or more residents, interns, and myself—a mere medical student—escort and squeeze upon each other to get as close as possible to the grand chief of thoracic surgery.

We walk through a ward hearing the chief describe the patients' conditions and operations. I notice a withered old man shuffling down the hallway wearing only his white cloth hospital gown. The master surgeon spots him with glee and announces a *first-ever* surgery that he'd just done on the patient, who he refers to not by name but by the novel operation for lung cancer: "And here is the world's first *DONUT MAN!*" he proudly exclaims.

He approaches the man from behind, pulls open the ties of his gown, and exposes him stark naked in the hallway—without his permission and in full view of staff and visitors. I walk around to the front of the patient to look at his face.

"I have succeeded in removing lung, tissue, and bone to produce the first Donut Man in history!" The chief of thoracic surgery puts his hand through a cannonball-sized hole in the patient's chest and wiggles his fingers on the other side. The entourage is amazed and cheers the work with applause.

The circus-freak patient without a name cannot speak. His head is bowed down in shame and the reflective glistening of teardrops fills his eyes.

I present a surprising exposé of the dark side of the founding fathers and mothers of alternative medicine.

GRANDEUR

Alternative medicine offered the possibility of greater empathy and creativity than the allopathic, or routine, medical field. I had to explore it, and fortunately, I met some wonderful and courageous healers within its broad space of creative genius. But the pioneer leaders in the field of alternative medicine are a different story…

It's my first day at a weekend seminar led by the famous, "Emmanuel" MD— who is in many ways the inventor of audiovisual media using imagery, visualization, and hypnosis. Emmanuel virtually created the self-help industry with tapes and videos: "Imagine Yourself Slim" and "Freedom From Pain." He had produced hundreds of glossy products and he had earned a good deal of money selling them. He had even begun to have a ghostwriter publish a 12-Step book for AIDS patients. That was because they were all helpless and addicted to sex or drugs, addicted to having AIDS, and they should just surrender to the disease.

"Good Morning," he says to the wide circle of about forty therapists and doctors in the room. "I AM EMMANUEL!" The intonation was reminiscent of a childhood memory: "I AM THE GREAT AND GRAND WIZARD OF OZ!" Emmanuel refers to the biblical origin of his name. "My name is the symbolic and prophetic name of the Messiah, prophesying that He would be born of a virgin and would be 'God with us.'"

I was impressed and attracted to his presence of ultra-confidence. I did not realize that he had a thoroughbred Narcissistic Personality Disorder. He was impressed with my Harvard credentials and my eagerness to help him. Soon, I became his junior colleague and saw the overflow of patients on his schedule. The clientele was packed with the names and personages of the rich, famous, and powerful.

I was hoping to find a mentor by working with Emmanuel. Perhaps I was also looking for a father figure. But he didn't have time for that; he had grand plans for himself, and what little time we had together over the course of almost two years was filled with his boastful vision. At first, my mentor's lack of support was disappointing. Then, it was disconcerting, as he only spoke to me twice in several months—but only to relay some absurd complaint from a patient.

"You have to *please* my clients, Michael. This wealthy lady was upset with you and I had to placate her," Emmanuel chastises me. The lady had just lost both her husband *and* an expensive ring in a fatal car accident where she was in the passenger seat. When she regained consciousness, she saw her husband's head impaled by a metal beam. Then, she noticed that she was missing the ring. She came in for immediate hypnosis to find out where the ring was, and was irked when I asked her about how she felt about the accident and her husband's death.

Emmanuel needed status and money. And he was terribly bombastic. He boasted that he was about to get a TV show on NBC that never transpired. He'd just been chatting with Ted Turner while seated beside him in his private jet…

And he had grandiose schemes.

He planned to run a "Clearinghouse" —a euphemism for a publishing company—where *all* creative work and products in *all* of alternative medicine would come to him and pass through him, from which he would extract a large percentage of the profits from others' labor.

As his codependent slave, I naturally obeyed Emmanuel's plan to bring all the pioneers together. But I soon found out how much they hated each other, and competed among themselves, marshalling their own followings and demanding allegiance to their private cliques.

Emmanuel's money-grabbing scheme was not well received.

Once or twice, my senior colleague seemed to listen to me. On one such rare occasion, he "heard" me describe my psychospiritual work and the incredible system that I'd been working on for ten years: Psychospiritual Integration, or "PSI." Nothing was dearer to my heart than this work, and I wanted to share my discoveries with my mentor…and to share part of my life's path and my Self, too.

After listening to me for a few minutes, he looked excited. I thought he was excited about my PSI healing process and discoveries. I imagined he was appreciating the wisdom and spiritual relevance of the work. He said, "Oh, good! Maybe *we* have a marketable product here!"

And then he changed the subject back to himself.

Slowly, I realized that Dr. Emmanuel's clear and primary motivation was not to serve and heal; in all his behavior, his goal was to attain acclaim and wealth. Exploitation was intrinsic to our arrangement; he would charge each patient I saw one hundred and seventy-five dollars for a fifty-minute visit; of that amount, I received sixty dollars. Whenever I had an open slot, one of his employees would rush to see me, crying and revealing the abuse she suffered working under Dr. Emmanuel.

When I realized that I was just an object in his world, I became depressed. Who better to see for therapy than *another* great and grand pioneer alternative healer? I chose to see the equally famous R.N. In the first therapy session, recorded on tape, Dr. R.N. lambasted Dr. Emmanuel with wrath and ire.

Her exact words were: "Well! You're not the *first* to come to me defecting from his camp! He thinks he's so good, but I'm far *better*. Maybe *he* can make an audience cry in ten minutes. *I* can make them cry in just five! And he charges one hundred seventy-five while I charge only one hundred twenty-five per hour—it's ROBBERY!"

I tried to excuse Dr. R.N.'s constant anger and explosive rage attacks as part of the side effects of steroid medications taken for her ulcerative colitis. But it was well known by all that worked with her that the judgmentalism and arrogance had always been her style.

She was the "tough, no-nonsense boss" and she was "always right." If I related a dream I'd had to her, just one sentence about my dream would lead to a fifteen-minute instant interpretation, which she was obstinately certain was the *only* interpretation, no discussion! Therapy consisted of her ranting and lecturing me, chastising and sometimes envying me—because those were the days when I *did* have money.

Like most Obsessive-Compulsive-Personality-disordered people with a narcissistic side, she had repressed her emotions so deeply that she was in denial of her obvious fury. One morning a bundle of cassette tapes that she used to tape the sessions arrived and the tapes were erroneously cut five minutes shorter than her usual fifty-five minutes. She took the first twenty minutes out of our therapy session to call and scream at the vendor, threatening to sue him. To any sane observer, she was having a tantrum. After hanging up, I mentioned how angry she must be. "I'm not *angry!* How absurd to say that! ... What's your problem?"

Then, I checked out working with the very famous and respected R.M. Again, he possessed the same narcissistic judgmentalism and rage, but also a Paranoid Personality Disorder that terrified his employees. They learned to shut up or fled from his office traumatized. I described my process of doing mind-body therapy, and my early work on shame and trauma…

He instantly scolded me, "How dare you see patients for psychotherapy for more than *six* visits! You should be ashamed!"

I met many pioneers in alternative medicine and they were mostly all the same: severely personality-disordered, narcissistically inclined, quasi-public figures that discouraged creative interaction. The roots of alternative medicine were planted by a unique brand of narcissists and profiteers without much conscience, as if the narcissistic imprint of their *prior* medical education was indelible. Almost all the big names in alternative medicine, the originals, were rogues, iconoclasts, and rebels *against* mainstream medicine. The early birds in alternative medicine *had* to be such personalities to defy the medical establishment and their aggressive traits were essential for success at the start of the bold movement.

Unfortunately, those understandable narcissistic and aggressive traits, which are required for individuation, had a downside: The pioneers of holistic and alternative medicine were intensely competitive with each other and behaved like eagles guarding their own nests. They instantly became rivals at the same time as their rapid rise to notoriety fed them a gluttonous diet of narcissistic supply. They were incapable of building a concerted movement that could follow their blazoned path.

A shocking exposé of the business control of the medical field by a handful of ruthless magnates is demonstrated in this true encounter, recorded verbatim.

BIG BUSINESS

By the 1990s, almost all the delivery of medical care had become subject to corporate ownership or to "the rule of the business model." Perverted ethics and corruption had conquered the last, lucrative field: the goldmine of interpersonal healing, itself.

I've been working as a temp doc, or *locum tenens*, for a month or so, in a remote village in the central valley of California. It's one of a large string of urgent care centers, often dubbed a "Doc-in-a-box" set-up. The centers specialize in Workman's Compensation injuries, and a shrewd and non-medically trained businessman, Mr. Roberts, owns them all. The physician at one of his sites in a coastal city left because he suffered severe burnout, so I was the chosen candidate to replace him.

But first, I must meet Mr. Roberts.

Mr. Roberts is a *secretive* man. The staff cautiously describes him as "a Southern gentleman." I drive up to a palatial building with marble colonnades nestled in the beautiful woods of Monterey. It's close to the famous 17-mile Drive, the land where Pebble Beach Golf Course is encircled by international billionaires' mansions, and where Mr. Roberts lives.

Three beautiful and impeccably well-dressed women in shiny high heels stand at the counter in the foyer. They are as perfect and poised as the Stepford Wives. I tell them that Mr. Roberts is expecting me now and they check his schedule. I'm asked, with formal courtesy, to take a seat. Mr. Roberts is a very *busy* man and I must wait for permission to see him at his convenience.

After half an hour, I ask one of the receptionists if I might see Mr. Roberts sometime soon. She nervously calls Mr. Roberts and then escorts me past a huge open bay containing perhaps a hundred workers, all altering and entering insurance billing data into computers at a ferocious speed.

The receptionist tells me certain rules about Mr. Roberts: "Do not greet him or shake his hand. Wait until he addresses you before you speak. Do not interrupt or disagree with him, he'll do all the talking. And, especially, do not try to negotiate with Mr. Roberts; he does *not* compromise."

She anxiously places her ear on Mr. Roberts's door and knocks softly. She meekly opens the door and pokes her head inside. Then, I am finally allowed to enter the ruler's sanctuary. Mr. Roberts is on the phone behind an enormous desk, dictating instructions to somebody. After about ten minutes, he hangs up and looks at me.

"So, you're interested in working for *ME*?"

"Yes, sir."

He commences a monologue, rattling off conditions of employment, expectations for performance, and tells me about his company. "Several *billion* dollars of annual revenue pass through my hands, King.

INDIVIDUATION

I own hospitals, I own private practices, and I tell doctors what to do and what *not* to do. I like running the surgeons—they make me richer. In fact, I own and run virtually the entire field of medicine for all central California. Just keep that in mind."

Mr. Roberts continues, "The urgent care part where you'll work isn't very profitable for me, but I'll keep it going for now. Because the Workman's Comp and urgent care boxes don't make much profit, I *deliberately* under-staff them."

He pauses and looks at me intensely. I've never had such a one-sided interview in my life and I'm speechless. But that's OK since I've been told to not talk anyway. Then he says, "Now, *GO!* See my staffing assistant. She'll give you paperwork to fill out. *Good-bye.*"

I walk out of the great and grand ruler's chambers and notice the faces of the anonymous army of scribes in the huge, un-partitioned, open bay. The workers appear solemn, silent and, except for a fretful frown, they are all expressionless. The hundred employees are hunched over at their computer stations. The only sound I hear is non-human, the muffled and furious tapping of keyboard buttons. I reminded myself of the universal staffing rule in clinical medicine today—the salaried business and billing personnel outnumber the actual providers of care by a ratio of *twenty* to one nowadays.

And then, my ordeal begins.

I am expected to see and treat forty to sixty patients in a ten-hour shift, which soon becomes fourteen hours without any breaks. I literally run from room to room, dashing about madly, for there are *nine* exam rooms and *nine* people to see simultaneously, plus the "bleeders" — lacerations, head trauma, two or three at once—laid out on cots in a tiny surgical bay.

The paperwork for Workman's Comp cases involves a detailed filling out of five to six long forms by hand. Anyone can walk in at any time for urgent care and the waiting room is always packed, especially at the closing hour. Patients with heart attacks, strokes, AIDS, ruptured ovarian cysts, MRSA, or any other grave illness or injury stumble into these "boxes" to save money compared with the cost of an emergency room visit. I have no medically trained colleagues, not even a physician assistant, to help me.

More patients seen, more profits.

Fewer medical providers, less expenses.

And the only thing that matters to my boss, the Czar of medicine, is the bottom line. The only "training" I receive is how to bill at the maximum level of service, even if fraudulent. It is mandatory, under constant pressure, to charge for "an approximate one hour with the patient," when, in fact, I only have a few minutes to spend with him or her.

It is also a rule to deny any treatment for Workman's Comp patients, other than billable on-site physical therapy, to the point that patients who are badly injured on the job must wait months to years to get the studies and surgeries they need. And they cannot survive on the meager income that Workman's Comp pays them.

For many providers, it's just a game of postponing *reparative* treatment until the condition is *irreparable* and permanent. Then, the injured worker can either get free treatment for the disability for life or a "cash settlement." The maximum amount of money they'd get for a broken spine, a lame leg, or a useless hand—for relentless pain treated with narcotics forever and never be fit to work again—is $8,000 to $10,000 in one single lump sum.

I am stationed in one of Mr. Roberts's urgent care boxes in Santa Cruz, California. I've just attended a meeting in a swanky restaurant with management last night. The meeting had two objectives: to pressure the doctors to bill at higher levels of service, and to simultaneously see more patients—thus shortening the length of time spent with each one.

The next day, my clinic manager interrupts the frenzy of my work to remind me to bill for the "max." I point to a national government guideline that is posted and affixed to the wall over my cramped desk; it outlines the estimated time required face-to-face for each billing category. I make her look at the legal guidelines: To bill for the level of service the management expects requires an average of one hour of patient interaction.

The regulation startles her and she frantically rushes to phone her supervisor. A few minutes later, she comes dashing back into my door-less office cubicle, nearly tripping over in her high heels, and rips the statute sheet down and tears it into pieces. "My supervisor told me to order you to ignore the government guidelines. You must focus instead on fabricating the correct number of pieces of data to justify the higher charges, and just disregard the time required to accomplish this feat."

I will hear the refrain many, many times during my routine medical assignments: "All we want are the numbers! Quality of care is irrelevant to the way medicine is practiced today!" The only form that a physician's many bosses care about is the billing form, called "the superbill."

A physician is a human being, and he or she cannot survive for long working at such an exhausting pace, filled with horrific bureaucratic hassles, in abysmal working conditions, and with grossly low pay per hour. The pressure to see more and more patients, faster and faster, has become unstoppable, irresponsible, and dangerous. It is to be anticipated that, with health reform, it will get much worse, for the medical profession simply does not fit into the business laws of "supply and demand."

I suffer severe burnout after a few months of working for Mr. Roberts and resign.

This is one of my most humorous, yet compelling, examples of flagrant greed and corruption in the medical field under business rule.

OFFICOUS AND VICIOUS

Soon after working in Mr. Robert's "Doc-in-a-box", I need money again and I am willing to consider stooping back down to working for another Worker's Comp and urgent care corporation where I'd worked briefly the year before. I know the game well: how to maximize profits and minimize care for injured workers. But my *heart* is wiser and stronger than my financially stressed ego.

The corporation has instituted a lengthy new training process for all employed and temporary, *per diem,* providers. The training contains nothing about the medical care of the worker; it is all brainwashing to make *sure* that the providers know how to push the profits to the top notch of the allowable maximum. The voluminous training manuals are filled with quotes…

"The average worker is usually in pain, anyway. Therefore, it is only reasonable to send them back to work in their familiar condition."

I've already gone through several unpaid days of this training, and the last part is to shadow a "model physician" and to learn how to use the profit-making skills that are built into the corporation's computer software. My emailed orders arrive: "You'll be shadowing Dr. Chang. She is the downtown San Francisco clinic's medical director. She is extremely knowledgeable about what it takes to be successful at Electra, Inc."

Dr. Chang is a short, plain looking Chinese-American woman with sore feet. She ignores me when I arrive, then silently points to a chair in her small office. I ask where I can put my bag and she replies, "Nowhere is safe here."

Then a suspicious grilling starts. "*SO*, you were doing internal medicine? That's useless here and will slow you down. You don't have to think here. It's systematized... How much urgent care and Worker's Comp have you done? ... *What?* You've already worked for us before? Then why am I wasting my time with you?"

She immediately calls the chief medical officer, incensed and ignoring me as I try to explain the new training protocol. I leave the room to take a deep breath while she yells into the phone. I feel suddenly nauseated; my premonitions warned me of this, and now my intuition confirms...

My inner voice whispers, 'This woman is cold and hostile, lacking the simple warmth and decency of social courtesy.' I return to the interrogation room.

"*SO*, you have a background in psychiatry? That's of no use here whatsoever! I wonder why they'd even *think* of hiring you. *SO!* What's *this* I see? You've done *alternative* medicine? I see it right here on your CV! That is *totally* not appropriate here! It's all bullshit nonsense!"

My inner voice whispers louder, 'This woman is abrasive and brusque, lacking the simple niceties and subtleties of the English language.'

The browbeating continues. "*SO*. Suppose you have a patient with acute low back pain. They are very resistant to going to physical therapy here. What is the correct thing to do?"

I answer that it all depends on the physical findings, the history, but that most likely anti-inflammatories, muscle relaxants, perhaps a mild narcotic analgesic, rest for a week without lifting, and then, maybe start physical therapy...

"NO, NO, NO! I said that she's *resistant*. She won't go to therapy and just complains. What do you do?"

I begin to describe a variety of cognitive-behavioral and interactive techniques that I've learned or invented, which have a very high success rate with resistant patients, and add that it's vital to *listen* to them, build rapport, and utilize the client-centered approach...

The medical director now has a wide-eyed expression of consummate contempt. With a tone of surly condescension, she blurts out, "You're so very sure of yourself, aren't you? *Nothing* you've said is correct. Now, the patient says that this has happened before and chiropractic treatments fixed it quickly, and she'd prefer to see a chiropractor rather than go to our in-house, billable physical therapy department. What do you do *NOW?*"

I answer that the patient's request sounds very reasonable, even though I know it's against company policy, so I'd...

"NO! She's resistant to physical therapy! You must *pound* her into going to physical therapy! You will deny all requests for chiropractic treatment. *You must punish her for being non-compliant!*"

Now, my inner voice is very loud, 'This doctor is heinous and sadistic! She's a lunatic!'

"*SO!* Another patient, same problem, but she's compliant with physical therapy, making some progress after six sessions in two weeks. What do you do *then?*"

I answer, though very defensively and stinging from the insulting harangue and the negation of everything I've said or tried to say so far, "Uh...I would continue physical therapy, since she's getting better?"

"NO, YOU FOOL! You authorize chiropractic treatment! *You reward her for being compliant with medical orders!*"

During the ordeal of the next three hours, Dr. Chang becomes progressively haughtier and, yes, *EVIL.* She shows me the medication cabinet and notices that there are only two bottles of one common drug left on the rack. She barks at a humble medical assistant, chastising him for being lazy.

"But, but...doctor, the shipment just came in and I am filling the meds up right now," he explains meekly.

She introduces me to an orthopedic surgeon who comes in twice a week. Even though I pick up his frustrated energy, I engage him in a lively, bonding conversation. Dr. Chang abruptly orders me, "Stop talking to him, *immediately!*" She adds that I'm not hired yet, so I'm not allowed to speak to any staff.

I sense that she's jealous of my ability to connect with people, something that she lacks. Later, the surgeon shows his own narcissistic side, bringing into Dr. Chang's office an X-ray report that he believes is incorrect. "Those stupid radiologists know *nothing,* I've had it up to here with them," he complains.

My teacher of the day, Dr. Chang, begins to tell me that work here involves a massive throng of urgent care, more than twenty-six patients per day on top of forty or more scheduled patients, and that it is all grueling work without breaks, on one's feet all day.

She rubs her feet.

Reports that take thirty minutes must be done in five minutes and no time is allotted for them. The super-rigged computer program to get top dollar payment takes weeks to learn, but I won't be given a single day. 'Why is she actively trying to discourage me from the job?' I wonder. Dr. Chang is on the phone, saying how unhappy she is about some issue…

'Perhaps she's just a really disgruntled employee.' I try to rationalize her behavior.

The marketing director staggers in. He's an unshaved GQ-looking man, sipping a soda, and bragging about getting new contracts. He leans backwards against the wall, and then lurches forwards over Dr. Chang's desk. He puts his arm around the waist of a female employee who comes into the room, almost kissing her.

'This place is a zoo!' I think.

I mention that I remember one doctor who works here; I'd met him a year ago. I don't mention that he was a nutcase archconservative who argued that Obama was the new Hitler and the world was ending. I can't remember his name, but I do mention that he's Greek, second generation; he'd told me that he was…Greek Orthodox.

"*Greek?*" Dr. Chang scowls mockingly. "There's no Greek working here. I've been the medical director here for four years and I'd know if somebody was Greek." The GQ guy says the doctor is indeed Greek and reminds me of his name.

"Oh, *him.*" Dr. Chang retorts. "If you'd said 'the short, fat and bald doctor,' I'd have known who you were talking about. Besides, he doesn't work here. He's *just* a temp employee like you will be, King."

An urgent care patient arrives. My orders are to shadow Dr. Chang, but she is increasingly suspicious of me. She says she doesn't want me to see her work. It would be, well, "interference." She relents. First, of course, Dr. Chang checks to see if the patient has insurance. "GOOD! I can bill for the max!" She smiles wickedly.

Warily, she lets me enter the exam room with her. Inside is a young woman, an out-of-town visitor to San Francisco, who is audibly wheezing and unable to speak full sentences. I immediately recognize that she has asthmatic bronchitis. Dr. Chang doesn't converse with the patient as she starts an automatic rapid-fire, belittling harangue on hygiene and covering one's mouth when coughing, washing hands…

I start to break the ice and establish rapport with the asthmatic. The patient instantly warms up, and senses that I'm "there for her." Dr.

Chang growls at me in front of the patient: "DON'T EVER, *EVER* INTERRUPT ME!"

The patient is pleading for support, but I keep quiet.

Dr. Chang has no patience for patients.

I watch Dr. Chang put her stethoscope on the patient's chest for a mini-second, diagnose a "cold," ignore the asthma, offer no medications or useful advice, and walk out the door in less than three minutes. "We'll get six hundred dollars for that one!" she chortles.

My role model continues. "A *good* doctor already knows exactly what the diagnosis is and what the treatment plan is going to be, before entering the room. What the patient says doesn't matter at all."

The next patient has a badly sprained ankle. It's a Worker's Comp case. Dr. Chang starts racking up the points in the wild goose-chase of signs and symptoms, each one worth a certain amount of money. Standing at the far opposite side of the room from the patient who is lying on a cot, Dr. Chang enumerates:

"No bruise..." The patient points to a bruise the size of a golf ball. "Ah! So— *Eccymosis present....*"

Her thoughts are along the lines of: 'That's *another* five-dollar finding. When I get six findings, it's an extra one hundred fifty dollars!'

"No swelling...." The patient, almost crying, points out that the injured ankle is twice the size of her other ankle. "Ah! So—*Edema present...."*

Dr. Chang walks over to glance at the ankle. *"Good circulation..."* She merely touches a toe with one finger, which cannot reveal circulation or pulse. She asks the patient to move her toes. *"Full range of movement..."* She does not check the movement of the sprained ankle at all.

She tells the worker to go to physical therapy, return in three days to see a doctor, then every week to see a doctor. Each will be recorded as "intermediate medical visits," claiming thirty to forty-five minutes face-to-face. In reality, the full few minutes are only used to dispense a handful of cheap medications and generate automated forms. The only form that helps the patient is one that limits what the patient can or cannot do at the job.

Dr. Chang walks out of the exam room in less than *two* minutes this time, and spends the next fifteen minutes doing the fraudulent billing game at her computer. Pulling down preset signs and symptoms, each one worth a certain dollar amount—of which none had been inquired about or examined at all—she selects the catchword phrases to warrant the equivalent of a *one-hour history and physical.* "I won't let some stupid high school bean counter cheat me out of *my* money!" she grumbles.

There are no patients waiting. It's time to abuse me again. "*SO*, why would somebody from *Harvard* Medical School want to work here?"

I look out the office door at the silent, submissive, and shamed faces of the staff that shuffles quietly by. I fade out and remember the day I'd worked here a year ago, and how the clinic manager made deprecating homophobic jokes about AIDS patients. I remember the many other "characters" that I've met at the corporation—a remarkable cluster of psychopathology. I'm thinking, 'Dr. Chang has Obsessive-Compulsive, Paranoid, *and* Narcissistic Personality Disorders combined—WOW! It's a rarity to have all three!'

She sees that another MD, a mignon under her, has not finished the computer charting from the day before. She fumes, "I've scolded her before! I will scold her again!"

My role model cannot reveal any vulnerability about herself, for she is a petty potentate with a Napoleonic complex. Her mockery intensifies. She *must* somehow beat me into submission. Her "case scenarios" slam me against the corner of a concrete wall of insult and derision. She must find fault with me, with everybody, with everything. That way, she can invalidate and ignore people, because people frighten her. Or, as with me, she must charge up to *attack and destroy* me as the rival that I represent in her sick psyche.

My inner voice commands me, 'If this woman is extolled as a paragon whose footsteps I am to follow…then those footsteps lead directly to hell.' I stand up, gather my things, and begin to walk out the door of Dr. Chang's office.

She's shocked. "Come back here! *Nobody* leaves me!"

"No, I'm not coming back. I used to be a professional trainer, Dr. Chang. I taught listening skills to the top executives of many corporations. The word doctor comes from the Latin *docere*, which means 'to teach.' And the first thing both a doctor and a teacher must learn is 'to listen.' I *refuse* to work for Electra, Inc.!" I declare loud enough for the staff outside Dr. Chang's office to hear.

Dr. Chang is left babbling for me to come back. "Come back, *nobody* leaves me! I *order* you to…."

I start shaking and waves of terrible rage beset me as I walk to the parking garage. I drive off, but I must pull over and park the car a few blocks away, just to try to get control of myself so I can drive home safely. My rage persists for three whole days. The end of hope for a career in traditional Western medicine is getting closer.

This medical piece depicts not only cruelty in the field of medicine, but touches upon the gross cruelty of the "criminal justice system." It has a vicious and sardonic humor.

EATEN ALIVE

The next job opportunity is working in a rural county jail in Stanislaus, California. They'd pay higher than I've ever earned, maybe over one hundred dollars per hour. Soon I meet the regional medical director, Dr. Gabri, who I mistake by voice and appearance for a man. She is brutally terse and cold, but she's politically well entrenched. She's also made a fortune off the jail business; nowadays she just flies around to supervise jail operations in three states.

The all-female clerical staff jokes as I am escorted out of the jail's medical office to be given a tour of the cellblocks. *'Don't feed the animals!'* they shout, cackling. I survey the beaten-down faces of the inmates and I begin to wonder if I am willing to return to my very roots of shame and trauma—a world where my survival is precarious.

Am I destined to do more work in the jail of my subconscious?

Must I focus a laser-sharp review on the prison of my past? Is it appropriate that I work in the place of *ultimate* abuse in America: the criminal justice system?

Torture in American jails and prisons was banned at San Quentin in 1940. Yet I know very well that physical torture persists in these places, and far more advanced torture by psychological trauma is a monster that seizes every inmate, every day, and in every way, imaginable.

Somebody who is not myself begins to rehearse for the series of interviews and interrogations that will take a week. I must pass the tests of a new recruiting agency, the for-profit medical franchising company, the medical director, the board of four women deputes, the sheriff, the FBI, and the mysterious and official "background check."

Dr. Gabri is militantly paranoid and domineering.

She makes it perfectly clear that the basic niceties of social intercourse are null and void. She barks out orders and crude warnings, compulsively asserting her superiority over me. I soon discover that, in the mind of my potential new superior, everything I do is worthy of criticism; the only proper behavior is none—*invisibility.*

'This could be the most treacherous and abusive job of my life.'

I fear for my soul as I rush to the downtown jail to meet with Dr. Gabri on the second day's orientation. She immediately orders me: "Take your tie off *now* and never wear it again! You will be strangled to death or an inmate will use it to commit suicide. You will *only* wear plain surgical scrub shirts from here on!"

She shoves me into a small, dark side-room in the antiquated men's jail, where guards still wear loops of huge keys dangling from their belts and there is scarcely space to breathe or light to see. Dr. Gabri commands me, "*Block* the door. *Sit* down. No! Don't take notes! Now *listen* very carefully and don't talk. Don't *ever*…." She speaks the same way to inmates. "*Sit!* Show me your foot. Take off your dirty sock. No! You can't…."

Dr. Gabri is as fierce as a tiger stalking its prey. "I want you to trust *nobody*. You must just be a shadow and do your work in silence. No smiling, no pleasantries, no chatting—*just do your work.*

"You will deny all non-acute medical care. You will be cold, terse, and unsympathetic to the inmates. Many uninsured inmates deliberately get arrested, thinking we'd take care of their medical conditions for free! *NO WAY!*

"You will ignore all chronic problems and diseases. It's too bad if they've got osteoarthritis, diabetes, cardiac disease, or disabling psychiatric problems. If they have asthma and want an inhaler, deny it too. They were out smoking like a chimney and must suffer the withdrawal and the consequences.

"And *don't flame it up.* They like lesbians working in jails but they're not partial to gay men. It's 'Don't ask, don't tell' here. And, by the way, I like your moustache…."

Then she spews out an endless roster of names, ranks, connections: who to trust, who to *not* trust, who will get what medical job done, who to appease to *not* block the medical orders…an infinity of powers that would rule over me and my practice of medicine. Next, she digresses to a list of pitfalls, landmines, red flags, and dangers. Dr. Gabri sums up her litany, growling, "If you are not *very*, *very* careful, and if you don't do *exactly* what I tell you to do—*they'll eat you alive in this place!*"

That is immediately confirmed in the next test: an interdisciplinary meeting. The chief Sergeant, a Mr. White, lambasts me after I introduce my background and myself. He flies into a rage when I mention Harvard.

Mr. White explodes saying, "You don't know anything. I have *two* Master's degrees and thirty years of experience. You have *nothing* to teach me. I'm your boss here and you can't do anything without my say-so!"

The Sergeant adds, yelling at the top of his capacity, "AND MY EGO IS BIGGER THAN THIS ROOM, DOCTOR!" The mad Sergeant spits out words like a machete hacking off my limbs.

"I don't *trust* you, I don't *like* you, and I'm *not on your side*. You've got to prove yourself to us. If you're *on our side*, maybe I'll trust you down the road. Then you can commit crimes and *do whatever*, and I'll defend you like family—just like I do for my loyal officers!"

I'm getting scared.

I'm getting *very* scared.

I'm being initiated into a mob, a gang, a Mafia.

The "allowable crimes" doubtlessly refer to the brutalization of inmates. I'm *consciously* willing to give the high-paying job a try, and attempt to hold on to my sanity and values, for as long as I can. But I know that my psyche has dug its subconscious heels in and will not budge. The queasiness in my gut compares the downtown jail to falling into a pit filled with vipers and poisonous spiders. Can I use this experience as "shock immersion therapy" to overcome my last strands of fear and shame?

I flash back to a forgotten bit of trivia…

In China, there is a long-standing ritual. Three beautiful virgins are put into a pit filled with cobras. They must be invisible to the snakes and not move or react when the vipers crawl over them. That's the only way to not be bitten. The one who survives the ordeal is festooned and celebrated; she is rewarded with gifts, money, and honor.

Now it's time for the "interview with the secretive panel of four women" at another site. Dr. Gabri orders me to sit in her expensive, rented Hummer. I must immediately obey, leaving my favorite tie lost inside the jail and critical material left in my parked car. As she speeds off, she makes me clean out the passenger seat by myself with nowhere to put sloshing plastic Starbucks coffee cups that roll at my feet. As I wait for the daunting interview in the antechamber of a large conference room, I read a poster on the wall.

By keeping our eyes focused on the light of optimism,
We can restore faith in ourselves and stay clear of the shadows.

Yet I see *only* shadows in this lugubrious, murky jail, and I am thinking I should stay clear of them before I become one of them. The conference room doors are flung open and Dr. Gabri signals me to come inside the special chamber. I impress the panel; I vow to save the taxpayer's money and make a profit for the franchised outfit that runs the delivery of medical services by denying medical care. I know the correct phrases to say and they are all lies. I give an eloquent speech to the intimidating women.

Afterwards, Dr. Gabri criticizes the speech for being too long and daring to suggest I had something to teach the jail staff. "Don't *ever* offer to do training for the non-medical staff. It implies that they don't know everything already."

'Perhaps, she's right,' I think, as I acknowledge my error. Correctional staff workers don't want any new information and they will discredit anything that's different from what they already believe and do. All they need to know is how to torture inmates. I recall the magazines in the rack of the antechamber outside the conference room—they featured articles on "Advanced Assault Tactics" and "Demoralization Techniques."

Dr. Gabri drives me back to my car at a furious and reckless speed, running over curbs and scratching the Hummer's fender. "I don't care. They won't see the damage." As she drives, she confides that her partner of twenty-plus years just died unexpectedly a few months ago, back on her huge ranch in southern Arizona. Not a *quiver* of vocal tone, nor *glint* of a tear, could betray Dr. Gabri's sentiments; it's just another fact without feeling.

'Was it *suicide?*' I suspect.

Fortunately, I fail the last hurdle.

The sheriff's and FBI's background checks reject me the next day and I am immediately escorted out of the jail. A sub-assistant tells me there's no way I'd be hired to work at the jail, *ever*. I wonder what they turned up, what skeleton was back in my closet? What supposed blemish from my past, stain on my character, sin of my soul, or betrayal by an enemy had blocked me from security clearance? Could it be my registered domestic partnership with a man? Or did my brother perpetrate yet another act of betrayal?

Or which one of dozens of petty potentates is prejudiced against me—in a flash, a word, an innuendo, or a gesture that they just didn't like? Was it the mention of "Harvard" and the Mad Sergeant? Was it that, in a lapse of caution, I'd commented to the director of human resources that I was writing a book, whereupon she looked horrified and asked me why I wanted the job?

I will never know and I don't care.

I am freed from the lion's den, the fangs of the dragon, and the corruption of my soul. I had averted the scratching, clenching talons and the thumping hoof beats of Satan, who had come very near indeed.

I had been *tempted* to sell my soul.

But I had been saved by grace of some fortunate stain on my past.

This longer excerpt is critical, representing my turning point away from the corruption and madness of the medical field. Character development, extreme depiction of the agony of a primary care MD, and succumbing temporarily to being a "typical doctor" all add gravity to this memoir.

ZERO TOLERANCE

It seems that the universe has determined that I must re-experience abusive environments and repeatedly approach sadistic people in a dependent posture, perhaps just to rehearse "saying no" and "getting out" sooner and sooner. It is ironic that I need money from *shame-inducing* employment to finish my books on shame.

I've always relied on one trustworthy agent to find jobs in the medical field, and I'm striking out on the few prospects she could scrounge up, like crumbs from the dinner table of the more fortunate. And the recession has given the business model and corporate control of the medical profession an excuse to finally and completely crush physician autonomy. Both "for-profit" business owners and "non-profit" managers in the *healthcare industry* (formerly known as the *medical field*) have found that despite a shortage of doctors, they can save money and increase profits by reducing their physician staff.

Some of the labor is shifted to midlevel providers, such as physician assistants or nurse practitioners, who are paid half the salary of a physician. But most of the savings come from forcing the remaining employed physicians to work at least *twice* as hard, *twice* the hours, and *twice* as fast across the board. There is no statutory protection to stop this abuse of physicians.

I thought I learned this in "My Last Job."

A *new* recruiting agent has been calling me for several months, offering undesirable jobs in undesirable locations. An opportunity to work with an indigent, Spanish-speaking population in the remote

Salinas valley comes up, and I decide to take it. My perfect fluency in Spanish, my cross-cultural experience, and my ability to deliver quality care in almost any aspect of outpatient medicine, from prenatal exams to geriatrics, will all be needed.

I am told that the previous physician, an Italian doctor, had been rude to the staff. He'd walked off the job, leaving it in chaos, on Friday, November 12th. I arrive on Monday, November 15th to a packed schedule and I am told to start working immediately.

The clinic is in a small house; there are three tiny exam rooms in former bedrooms. It is in the *poorest* city of *wealthy* Monterey County, with a massive unemployment rate of nearly fifty percent. The Hispanic workers depend on seasonal agricultural labor, and, it's wintertime. Furthermore, many food-supply companies like Dole have laid off their manual field hands and factory workers—ironically "putting them on the dole."

Instant red flags flash before my eyes as I look inside the massive, disorganized, and illegible charts. It's a replay of my last job, only worse. Most of the patients have diabetes, hypertension, high cholesterol, and triglyceride levels and chronic pain due to the cumulative effect of years of grueling labor on the musculoskeletal system. I realize that these poor Mexican workers replicate the stress and strain of historical slaves, who probably suffered the same diseases in centuries past.

I begin to charm the staff of five bilingual Hispanic women, all of whom are in their 20s. My two medical assistants have only had a high-school-level crash course in very basic medicine, focused on taking vital signs and performing simple procedures. I know that I need their political and logistical support and that their morale is very low. I also know that their instant impressions and rumors about me will quickly go up the chain of command, and that mere gossip and mistaken impressions could easily get me fired.

But there's no time to bond with the "girls." The flood of appointments, double-booked for every ten-minute slot, nonstop throughout the day, keeps me rushing, cramming, treating, and bonding with the patients—all of whom are new to me. My humanitarian ethics combines superb quality of care with the goal of boosting the self-esteem of every person with whom I interact.

But nowadays…

I receive no training at all about the clinic's idiosyncratic protocols, which require different paperwork from prescription pads to billing sheets for over a half-dozen categories of billable-to-insurance or cash-paying patients. In fact, I have no contact whatsoever with the clinic manager, any administrator that rules over me or any other provider for over a week.

No midlevel or higher-trained staff, no Internet access for vital medical information and patient education, no specialists to consult about obscure and extraordinary ailments…*nothing* is provided—not even paper clips. I work hard and fast, into the evenings and over the entire first weekend, to try to catch up.

There are stacks of un-reviewed charts with critical lab results, as well as emergency room, critical care, and intensive care unit discharge orders—and life-saving prescription refill requests that have just been ignored for weeks.

When I get to my motel after each workday, I collapse, *pounding* the pillows with tears of frustration. 'How can I physically survive and keep my ethics in this job?'

The answer was to come later: '**I can't**.'

I am breathless, bent over, and pouring through a three-hundred-page chart about a patient who hasn't been seen in two years. He's missed six appointments since then. Three other patients have been sitting in the other two exam rooms, where they've been waiting for an hour already.

I glance at the progress notes and the prior physicians' entries are illegible. I quickly look at the old labs and later connect them to the empty medication bottles the patient brought in. These are the *only* clues I'll have about the patient's diagnoses. Before entering the exam room, my dry, unwashed fingers flip through the "correspondence" section to skim over consultations, discharge summaries, and disability forms. A picture begins to form in my mind, although vague and convoluted:

Morbid obesity…

Gout, *uncontrolled*…

Diabetes, *uncontrolled*…

Hypertension, *uncontrolled*…

Lipids, *uncontrolled*…

Renal Failure, *unmonitored*…

Strokes, *leading to dementia*…

Coronary Artery Disease, with stenting after a heart attack, *but the patient can't afford anticoagulants*…

Neuropathy, with numbness and pain in the feet and hands, *which sting and burn like lit matches*…

Retinopathy, with glaucoma, retinal detachment, intra-ocular hemorrhage, blindness, *all untreated*…

Low thyroid, emphysema, blood in stool, anemia, cirrhosis of the liver, osteoporosis, arthritis…
CHRONIC PAIN AND DEPRESSION…

The medical assistant records the single complaint of mere "heartburn" for which I've been given a generous ten-minute slot. I now have only five minutes left.

I take a deep breath and knock on the door. I enter the exam room and warmly greet the patient in Spanish. An elderly lady with a grim face, annoyed for having had to wait an hour, stares at me. "Why can't I see the same doctor I saw before? I *never* see the same one."

I apologize for the delay and the physician turnover, and then I notice the patient is coughing. She spits blood-tinged sputum onto a handkerchief.

"My knees hurt and I want injections in *both* today, before going to Mexico for three months to see my dying son. I'll need written refills of the fourteen medications to last for that long."

It's useless to address the chronic, life-threatening diseases with her, because she is illiterate and simply can't understand her role in the prevention of morbidity without a dedicated health educator who could spend hours with her. I look at the empty pill bottles; there are two bottles of the same drug and she says she takes one of each daily—*it's an overdose.*

I show her the bottle for an *essential* medication for her diabetes. "Oh, I don't take *that* pill. It's too big, so it's too strong, and that's why I have heartburn," she reasons.

I chat with the patient as I try to get some history and do a physical exam. I must collect an average of two thousand bits of data in less than three minutes now. I must forget preventative protocols— mammogram, Pap smear, bone density studies, colonoscopy, and vaccinations. I must forget *most* studies and labs because they're too expensive for her.

I try to fill out lengthy referral forms and prior authorization forms for optometry, orthopedics, pulmonary, podiatry, and mental health. But I know in advance that no orthopedic surgeon, pulmonologist, endocrinologist, gastroenterologist, or other specialist is likely to be willing to see poor patients or do diagnostic procedures for them.

I scribble a few notes that will be legible for the *next* physician to use. I try to update the problem and medication lists. My hand hurts as I spin out a dozen prescriptions and check off codes on the "super-bill" and a dozen other forms.

"I also need a letter stating that I must take a three-month leave for medical reasons. I MUST SEE MY SON!" She starts to cry. I console her grief and put my arm over her shoulders.

"No problem. I'll write the letter."

This will put me another ten minutes behind.

Previous physicians have berated her about her diet and lack of "follow through." So, I flatter the lady and invoke her trust. I crack a joke in Spanish, I cheer her mood, and I attain a semblance of empathy and rapport. My intuitive wisdom chooses just the right moment to insert a hypnotic message of hope and faith in a positive outcome: "YOU CAN DO IT!"

I am attuned to the angst of her soul, which longs for a life better than poverty and the diet of sugar and fat that comes with it, and which also longs for reunion with her displaced family and her familiar native land and mores. I know that her many decades of life in America, with its relentless stress imposed on the weakest and poorest of the population, have worn her down. America's interpersonal coldness and exploitative Narcissism are combined with a lifetime of hard physical labor. It's a deadly potion that has wrought irreversible havoc to her body.

But today, she will leave with a good impression of both herself and me. And I will leave the room exhausted, only to be besieged by phone calls from pharmacists, employers, consultants, and therapists; mountains of mandatory signatures pushed at me by staff, with no idea what I'm signing; more critical lab reports and refills—often for narcotics with clear evidence of drug abuse; and incessant *questions, questions, questions…*

Then I rush into the next room and repeat the impossible.

After the first week at the clinic, word about me had spread in two dramatically divergent paths. The *patients* passed the word that there was a "good" doctor in the little clinic and more and more lined up to see me. The *staff* passed the word that I was "too slow" and patients complained to them in the waiting room. The repercussions that followed were swift, predictable, and tragically familiar.

The schism between quality versus quantity, or the practice of clinical medicine versus the business model, leans heavily on the latter in both categories. I am secretly investigated for "numbers of patients seen" and "time per patient." I am failing on both criminal accusations after only three days at the new job.

The most damning fault was that I'd spent an entire *hour* with one patient on one day. He was a young man with deadly diabetic ketoacidosis, flesh-eating Staph all over his scalp and armpits, and who was also a narcotic addict and a depressed, suicidal sociopath.

I'd saved his life.

My 9th day of temp work...

The unseen, unknown chief operating officer known as "Ruthless Ruth" calls the placement agency. She tells them to force me to see more than thirty complex patients per day and to *also* send a replacement for me as soon as possible. I am being put on probation and fired at the same time. My new agent calls me and says that I could *easily* be replaced. "I've got at least five doctors ready to take your job. You're nobody special. You better work harder and faster, or else...."

The unmet CEO, who is also my medical director, comes to the clinic to check into the situation. Dr. Moreno is wearing a drab three-piece brown suit. He is a short, skinny Hispanic man with a pale, mottled face and a grimacing countenance of haughty disgruntlement. I present my case for quality of care and a more lenient number of patients per shift in a diplomatic, or perhaps *placating*, manner.

Dr. Moreno seems to verbally support me. "It's true that King City is the most difficult practice in my entire chain of clinics. It's a solo practice, it's by far the poorest city in the county, and the job involves very complex internal medicine." I think I hear him mumble, "Thus, *nine* patients per *four-hour* shift would be reasonable."

But he wavers. With a brutally harsh tone of voice, he says, "When I supervised residents doing their clinic rotations, they'd bring me a five-page summary on the patients. *I'd rip it into shreds and throw it at their faces,* saying, "You've got *one minute* to tell me the problem and treatment plan!" He adds, speaking louder with presumptuous pride, "I give nationwide medical lectures on the **'eight-minute rule.'** If you *ever* spend more than eight minutes with *any* patient, you're wasting time and money!"

I protest in debate. "But studies by the AMA and others have shown that it takes *thirty* minutes to see an educated, insured, middle-class patient with just *one* problem! And here, the patients have an average of five serious chronic problems, three acute problems, and *no* continuity of care at all!"

He responds haughtily, "Those studies were *fraudulent!* They were only engineered by liberals to protest against HMOs!" It is useless to argue with Dr. Moreno because Dr. Moreno is argumentative. His mandates are dictatorial, arbitrary, and inflexible. He ignores feedback from his front-line providers who languish under his whip.

He jeers, "*All* my physicians complain about the workload. They *beg* for mercy. But medicine has changed. The future will be even *more* challenging when the plans for universal healthcare increase demand by four hundred percent with a fixed supply of physicians!"

I acquiesce and describe, from a business standpoint, how I am strategically advertising the clinic to local enterprises. I mention that I've called the owner of a popular gym and gotten her willingness to take on motivated patients for free aerobic fitness coaching. I'd then sent her a glowing letter of gratitude, *boasting* a bit about the clinic and *boosting* her profile of "commitment to optimal health." It's the sort of letter that she'd post in the window as an advertisement for her gym, a win-win deal for both businesses.

Then I explain how a few extra minutes of quality care for patients creates word-of-mouth advertising; it could attract more insured and middle-class patients, which would offset the mix of indigent or MediCal versus privately insured or cash-paying patients…thus leading to a more profitable practice.

Now I make my plea for support.

"Look at the reality. This is a solo practice without peer or midlevel assistance. There are patients who've been coming here for ten years and *never* got a work-up for grave diseases. Not only are there language and literacy barriers, but they also have *multiple* organ failures, requiring that I practice *everything that exists in the field of medicine*, from primary care to acute care to virtually all the medical and surgical subspecialties. In fact, I represent a full panel of specialists fused into one."

WHY CAN'T I SEE THE OBVIOUS?

Dr. Moreno is impressed by my eloquent appeal and leaves the *fifteen*-minute meeting appeased. But I check my schedule the next day—I am still double-booked for two months ahead. The "no-show" rate is dropping due to my reputation of only one week. There are urgent follow-ups, squeeze-in visits for gravely ill patients I've already just seen, and new patients lining up with acute problems demanding treatment. I'm frantically triaging throngs of patients packed in the hallway and realize it is imperative to see at least half of the drop-ins.

On my twelfth day of temp work, the usually absent clinic manager saunters into the clinic in the late morning, and I need to clarify the "quantity" issue which has apparently been ignored. I ask the manager,

"Didn't Dr. Moreno limit my load to nine patients per shift? That was *my* understanding."

"NO!" she exclaims. She is obviously irritated by the question. "He said nine to *twelve* per four-hour shift, aiming for more like *thirty patients per day*. He said it twice to me! You obviously weren't listening to him in your short meeting! We had a *thirty*-minute meeting about it afterwards."

My morale vanishes as I fragment into another breaking point. I feel unappreciated, abused, and threatened by hostile management. I am being forced to be an accomplice to malpractice in violation of both my ethics and the law. My two superiors, the chief operating officer and the medical director–CEO, are both mentally ill.

"We offer access to care, but not quality of care!"
"From now on, you will not get paid for overtime hours!"
"You will be judged by your numbers, not by patient satisfaction!"
"One problem per visit and have them come back infinite times to address their problem list."
"Medicine is a business."

I decide to try an unprecedented experiment: I will practice medicine as the management demands. My shame and anger turn into hatred. I cannot bear being discounted and exploited by all the management as a replaceable object anymore. The hatred is so powerful and deep that it cannot be contained. It generalizes to hating not only my abusers, but hating the job, and then, for the first time in my life, *I hate the patients.*

In desperation, I begin to dread their expectations that render it impossible for me to have a sustainable existence. I can no longer *not* have time to wash my hands, to use the toilet, or to eat. In madness, I envision the patients as my enemies that put both my physical and economic survival in jeopardy.

I morph into a medical monster. Under management's dictates, patients are to be denied help and refused treatment. They are to be cajoled and controlled. I flash back to the last time I'd seen a doctor for my *own* healthcare. It was during my last job, when I'd developed hypertension and an abnormal EKG due to stress. I told the young physician about the workload of four doctors that was dumped on my sole shoulders. He chastised me, saying that I must refuse to treat the patients so well. "They'll eat you alive in this field!" he said, just like Dr. Gabri's words at the jail.

INDIVIDUATION

My hands are now blocked from *touching* the patients, unless absolutely necessary. They might have an infectious disease and I don't have time to wash them. No handshake greetings or farewells—just a perfunctory exam by a stethoscope that *might* listen to their heart and lungs.

Rapport is gone as I do the paperwork in the exam room so that the patients can see *how much work* they cost me and so that I can avoid the interruptions of the outside staff and phone calls. If they speak to me while I'm writing, I signal them to be quiet and *never interrupt me.*

My boundaries are tough, cold, and rude. My limits are strictly minimalistic as I, too, only scribble notes in the charts. No time for chatter or fun, not even with the frightened children who come in for a "well-child check." There's no time for a physical exam; I'll just pretend I did it to cover my ass, like everybody else. I fixate, 'I must get through them quickly!' This is my *only* objective. No time to console the grieving, calm the anxious, or educate the ignorant.

"I have a pounding left-sided headache with momentary blindness," a patient complains. Do I dare start a work-up for an impending stroke? *Nope.*

"I waited thirty minutes and I've got to get to work by noon...." I tell the patient that I've already spent *twice* the allowed time with her and I'm liable to being fired for this.

Then the hatred generalizes to its inevitable destination: *I begin to hate myself.* I hate myself for practicing medicine as ordered, in negligence of my training and values, in opposition to innumerable supervisory, governing, and auditing agencies, and without empathy or caring.

The next day, the medical director–CEO arrives with an impressive entourage. The clinic manager and a medley of both potentates and peons cluster around me at my cramped little desk in the open bay where all the staff and patients can hear. Only Dr. Moreno sits down. He stares at me squint-eyed and then asks me two questions.

First, he asks, "I want to know if the *patients* are satisfied with your care." I suspect that a patient has complained about my new style of treatment.

"I don't know for sure," I answer cautiously.

Then he asks me, "I want to know if *you're* happy with the job."

I must say the truth, even though I am fully aware of the consequences. "Well, actually, I'm *not* happy with the job."

I explain, once again, that the load of thirty or more patients per day is excessive, impossible, drastically reduces the quality of care, and leaves no time whatsoever for my hefty administrative and other non-direct patient care duties. Holding onto the vestigial veneer of my ethics, I limit my disagreement to one *professional* point: "We appear to have a basic difference of opinion regarding your eight-minute maximum rule."

Dr. Moreno's usual disgruntled visage contorts into a snarl of disgust. He rams his rolling chair hard backwards, banging against the opposing wall with such force that the plaster cracks. His concert of followers stands around us in shocked silence. Nobody has *ever* dared disagree with Dr. Moreno…

Dr. Moreno's rebuttal is in the form of a hysterical, global, and *personal* attack. "You think *thirty* is something excessive? You don't know anything at all. You don't know this county! Private practice doctors here easily see thirty per day. And they'd see *forty or fifty* if they could get them! This is *nothing* compared to other clinics here or nationwide. You are ignorant about the future of medicine. *Business* rules the whole field and only the *numbers* matter! Do you hear me? *ONLY THE NUMBERS!*" Then he adds, "Besides, you have *no experience* in a private practice!"

"But that's not true," I protest. "I had a private practice for twenty years and unfortunately, because of insurance companies and HMOs, at the end only the rich could see me, and—"

"**HA!**" He scoffs loudly, waving his hand imperiously to the on-lookers. I've slipped by using the word "rich" and now Dr. Moreno plays it up to his audience. "Then what the *hell* are you doing *here?*"

"I guess I have to decide whether to stay here or leave," I answer solemnly.

Dr. Moreno lowers his head and his tone of voice, "Well, that's up to you…."

During an agonizing moment of reflection that seems an eternity, I calculate *another* type of a thousand variables and concluded that my survival here is worse than precarious; Dr. Moreno's psychiatric illness of paranoid, fanatical Narcissism has turned on me as a *rival* to be destroyed. I've been through all this misery before; every detail has been replicated and magnified to test me.

I reply, "I quit."

I snap back to myself again.

I had *attempted* to sell my soul.

But this time my own mind and body saved me.

LET THE CAGED LION ROAR!

INDIVIDUATION

LET ICARUS DEFY THE SUN AND THE SEA!
LET THE DRUMS BEAT SAVAGE AND WILD!

SUDDENLY THE ANCESTRAL DRUMBEATS STOP

SEQUENCE FIVE: IDENTITY CLOSURE

This analogy between slavery and writing is more sophisticated, stemming from the genre of "writing about writing".

SOLIPSISTIC WRITING

Slave-based behaviors are creeping into my process of writing. Passing on a legacy of Narcissism, like that of my rebellious field slave ancestors, and enmeshing with or being possessed by another, like my obedient house slave ancestors, is not limited to human relationships. I have begun to realize that it can happen during a creative process, too. I am tempted to engulf the book as the book is engulfing me.

After the epiphany of three weeks ago, the "**SNAP**," one hundred pages of text, plus fifty narrative pages about all my relationships, spanning a third of a century, blasted out like dynamite. I'd flung open the deepest crypts of my traumatic memories, resolved eighty percent of my post-traumatic stress, and erased the terrible flashbacks....

Then, I just stopped writing.

Shock? Exhaustion?

I produced nothing for the next two weeks—ZEAL ZERO.

It was as if my rowboat had run into a shoal or a reef, and I began to think that I'd have to paddle a long, long way around it before ever making progress toward the Silver City again. I surrendered to being stuck on the shoal and motionless on the barnacled reef. The flow of writing had slipped from my control, from flood to drought.

I'd become narcoleptic when trying to write; it wasn't like normal sleep. I would just sit at my desk and space out. Then, I found myself napping, gardening, listening to music, beautifying my apartment, and daydreaming. For a while, it was OK, even enjoyable. I was contented and relaxed.

The book is my own brain: evolving, growing, self-correcting, and self-healing. When I sped through the voluminous span of one hundred and fifty pages, I did not respect my brain and I crashed into writer's burnout. My mind could not process so much, so quickly.

I RISK BEING ENSLAVED TO PLEASING THE READERS AS MY MASTERS.

The dreaded codependent anxiety has resurfaced. I now feel concern for the reader of this book, the unknown and imaginary person who I want to protect from being abused by this book. I want to shelter him or her from any harm that may be imparted, and from any painful knowledge that may be gleaned.

I want my book to be a good child and do no harm. Will it behave well when I release it? I want to serve the reader, to help, heal, and inspire him or her. I do not want to bore, depress, or enrage him or her. I fear I may over-tax the reader's own brain.

Perhaps the book is too long, intense, and deep. But is that not the nature of a meaningful life? And, therefore, is it not also the nature of a meaningful book *about* my life? The book is a journey, even a saga, through my life and beyond. It does not exist inside the "theme park" of entertaining and easily digestible reading.

The most troubling and paradoxical question about abuse appears to be: Is it abusive to expose abuse? Is it cruel to obliterate the veils of ignorance that some people seem to need? Certainly, my parents protest that I abuse them by exposing their abusing me. I abuse them when I say I feel abused, or ask them to stop the abuse, or even mention the *word*, "abuse."

When my parents react to "abuse," they are not saying that I have done an action that has abused them. What they are truly saying is that they are experiencing an emotional response to the word itself. They hear it as a complaint or an accusation, and they feel shame, hurt, or disgrace.

By tradition, abuse is a private matter, more private than the graphic details of one's sex life. Abuse is a secret matter, not to be broached anywhere, with anybody, under any circumstances, unless one is in therapy or a criminal investigation is invoked. There is a stubborn cultural legacy, based in folk law and folklore that "abuse" must be kept in a subconscious cage. And that's how abuse remains alive.

I RISK BECOMING A SLAVE TO THE BOOK.

It has also dawned on me that the book is becoming abusive to me like a narcissistic predator. It seems to demand *all* of me, *all* the time. At what point did I lose my individuality and independent lifestyle to it?

When and how did I become an extension of the book, slaving for the book, without a sense of Self? I fear that I may lose my own identity by becoming enmeshed with an independent entity. I, Michael, the writer, am at risk of becoming I, "Hide and Play Dead," the book.

Last night, the book crept in and spoke to me, "You've had your break. Now, this is resistance! You are giving up and you will never finish me! You will fall on the racetrack, just before reaching the finish line again. You must blast again through my remaining chapters."

THE ANCESTRAL DRUMBEAT RESUMES IN CHAOTIC DISHARMONY

"No time for more than one meal a day. No time for exercise or walks in the spring sunshine. It's worth risking your health to continue full steam. Once the writing is done, proofread and perfect, succinct to nearly blunt, no wasted words, no digressive fillers, assured that all is top quality, marketable and saleable… NO! Not even *then* can you relax and enjoy life.

"You must revise me with outside advice and editing. You must also start writing my sequel, a second book with all the unused text and stories, and you must start to prepare talks and a lecture series and rehearse for media appearances, immediately upon finishing *this* me."

I abruptly ceased to allow myself to enjoy the creative process. The sadistic book invoked my masochistic self-abuse, and justified whipping and beating myself out of all I've discovered—the *re-discovered* resources of relaxation, contentment, and faith.

Against my heart's yearning and rebuking my epiphany, a field slave mandate was issued: There is no time for rest, recuperation, recreation, and re-creation of Self anymore. Not until the harvest is done. Not until the book is finished. Not until the book is born, grown up, and presented to the world.

Then, I remembered the adage: It's the journey, not the destination. My inner voice said, "You must have a social life. You're getting cabin fever. You're lonely. You need to meet a new coterie of peers, creative people, and writers. Maybe join a writer's support group, like those offered at 'Book Passages.' You must take better care of your body; listen to it and slow down, for God's sake!"

I am torn. Should I continue to sacrifice the healthy balance of my physical life for the emotional progress that comes from my writing? Can I chart a moderate course and not overindulge in the "slavish" work of fathering the book?

I RISK MAKING THE BOOK MY SLAVE-CHILD

I confess that I have begun to be solipsistic and abuse my book-child, just as I had been abused, and my mother had been abused, and all my ancestors abused, back through the many centuries of subjugation.

"She was to get right to the finish line under any or all types of pressure necessary to produce an offspring that her father could 'show off' to the world."

I want my book-child to dispense with the slow birthing process and I am trying to push the baby out prematurely. I almost want a cesarean section to deliver a fetus that is just in the beginning of its third trimester of gestation. Then, I want my book to grow up, now! There is no time for playing with or enjoying my book as a child.

Raising a book is a serious venture. He cannot be allowed to take a form or to mature independently of my machinations. I distrust his innate will and unknown destiny. I want to possess him. I also want to protect my young book from outside influences. I don't want other opinions to pervert my adolescent book. I resist allowing my offspring being handed over to the unknown hands of editors, critics, or readers. I want him all to myself: "Don't touch my child!"

He must metamorphose into a finished adult, *quickly!* I want to control and manipulate my adult book and maybe its readers, too. I am constantly nagging and correcting him: "You're too long! You're too deep! You're too technical!" It's my duty to mold and form it, and to make it perfect.

I am so tempted to exploit my book-child. It is true that, sometimes, the book appears to be an extension of myself that belongs to me as my object. I expect my book to give me the resources that I don't have on my own and to accrue to my self-esteem. I want him to prove my worthiness to my parents and to gain full independence from them. He will provide me with strong boundaries, like a fortress in which I will be able to hide my vulnerabilities.

I need him for my own financial survival, like a peasant raising many children and expecting them to pave the way to his retirement. Against my conscious scruples, I am also guilty of writing with the agenda of attaining freedom from the abusive working conditions in the ever more corrupt state of the current medical profession.

INDIVIDUATION

I expect my book to bring me status and recognition, meaning and, yes, even love to my life. He will attract potential partners like a matchmaker magnet. He is going to give me a positive life experience and a fresh direction for my career. Because of my perfect book's anticipated success, I will finally have self-esteem.

"Her father had an agenda for his offspring: He wanted to prove something to the world that had looked down on him. He wanted to make his daughter a prodigy— to accrue to his voracious shame-based ego."

But I also know that the resources that I seek cannot come from exploiting *things*; they can only come from loving *people*, whose respect, support, and devotion I may someday internalize as self-love.

If I exploit the book, my child will end up *contrived*, not created. Books are like living beings with separate and freely chosen selves and identities. I must not boss, bash, and hammer out my child's performance and eventual future with unrealistic deadlines and selfish expectations.

Solipsism involves a narcissistic attempt to control the outcome of events and things that are truly independent of one, and whose fate is unknown. It's rigging the vote or deciding the outcome of a study or experiment before doing it. It's like bad psychotherapy that fashions others into preset and preconceived models of normalcy.

This is my first book, and writing it is the single most daunting and massive challenge of my entire life. It is the story of my life! It is also like my first and only child—the child I never had. The newborn book-child inherits half of my "genome," but the other half comes from "beyond." And my grown-up book will survive past my death...

A great musician lets his or her instrument perform, surrendering to the piano or the violin; the interpretation of the score is as unique as each performance. Although there are "precise sciences," even mathematics evolves when the premises and formulas are reconfigured. There are so many variables and unknowns in life; one such variable is "time" and the other is "form." To force them to become controlled and predictable constants is narcissistic. They have an intrinsic right to remain variables.

Perhaps, writing is the reverse of a race? You don't speed up nearing the finish line; you slow down to marvel and contemplate the birth of a complete work. The book is now emerging into form, uncovering meaning and revealing thematic truths that are different than I had anticipated. I know that I have the pieces to the puzzle of the book, but I still can't discern what the final picture will be. Just as I have the pieces of my true Self, without knowing how I will emerge, either.

One cannot control either time or form of a creative process.

It is sacrosanct.

One cannot control either time or form of a child born to oneself.

He or she is sacred.

But I must face a somber reality: The business model *will* intrude solipsistically into the realm of writing and plot the arena of human creativity. Its nature is to objectify and exploit people and their products from the perspective of their "value" to amass money in the publishing industry marketplace. But all the books I shall write are living, independent creatures, and nobody can destroy their primary identity or their life's meaning and purpose. No agent or publisher can suppress the true and unique selves of the written words. I will always be the books' father and love them. And, I will always speak my Truth through the medium of the books and public forums. The worth of the books is the worth of my own integrity.

"I AM A VOICE!"

I must reframe the expected events that threaten to subvert my mission. I perceive that this book and its sequels have a sacred, not selfish, purpose; they are sent out as missionaries and are about to enter a strange land, with the noble ideal of changing the world. Or, they are emissaries to a foreign court, with a priceless message and a prophetic warning.

Soon, I envision the current book, my first child, as almost a young adult and ready for college. He or she will apply to schools, in the form of agents and publishing houses; if accepted, he or she will have new teachers and mentors as I fade into the background. In any case, I must let the adult book follow its own course. As in the Buddhist philosophy of "independent arising," the Book faces a destiny of surprises and mysteries that I cannot foresee.

Can I change my perspective back to my epiphany of three weeks ago? Can I truly allow this natural creative process of form and time? Can I relinquish my temptations to dominate, control and forge the book, the readers, and myself? Can I permit the **Book**—my child—the **Readers**—themselves—and **Me**—myself—to manifest independent thought forms and pursue divergent paths?

I am not the Book: It is an independent life form of consciousness. I merely helped conceive the book, with other forces involved. The book is now rapidly becoming a separate and free entity. I have confidence in it and I'm sure it can cope with life's challenges, as can I. It will fend for itself in the unknown world of its future. And the reader will protect him or herself, too.

There is a natural time span for the book, my brain, the readers, and our interdependent destinies. There is uncertainly and mystery about the creative process. I did not even plan to write this segment about how narcissistic and self-absorbed, how controlling and exploitative, the creative process of writing can become, because I just didn't recognize it at first.

If I truly love my child, the book, I will allow it to finish itself and proceed ahead in ways that I cannot predict. If I truly love my child, the book, I must give it support and guidance, but see it as a separate entity with a unique destiny, and not an extension of myself. If I truly love myself, I will allow my brain to evolve and heal at its own pace and in unpredictable ways, too. My mother lives with the "comfortable certainty" of death. I live with the "uncomfortable uncertainty" of a creative birth, a natural growing up of form, in its own time, in its own way.

THE DRUMBEATS SLOW DOWN AND LIGHTEN UP

This trilogy of narrative dialogues with my mother and, in the third, with each of my family members, demonstrates my mother's persistent toxic suppression of my individuation (solipsism), and chronic depression. It captures the never-ending role of my mother as my primary antagonist in the nonfiction novel. The third piece represents the absurd epitome of my entire family's repudiation of my attempt to individuate and heal from PTSD by writing this book.

YOURE DEAD

The phone rang the special tone reserved for my parents. I always need to brace myself when they call, and the ring-tone triggers an alerted state.

"Oh, Hi, Mom. How are you doing?" I politely inquire.

My mother blasts out with venomous rage, "I assume you're dead!"

"I'm sorry, Mom, I don't understand. What are you trying to say?"

"I assume you're *dead,*" she repeats, louder, in hot hate. Then she bellows, "And I'm just *fine* with it!" I feel slapped and stabbed by the cold hate of my erasure.

I hear the true message: You haven't called me in over a week and I feel like I'm losing control over you. I'm losing you to a book that will expose me and I hate you for exposing me. Although it is I who is afraid of dying, you are my other self; therefore, I will project my fear of imminent death onto you. Furthermore, I *wish* you were dead, because you are becoming the bad, prodigal son again!

"I ASSUME YOU'RE DEAD!" she screams again, for the third time. I refuse to act frightened by her threatening and violent innuendoes. I tell her that she sounds depressed, but I'm just fine and I don't know why she's so upset.

"You could die any day now! You're at the age when you could have a heart attack or a stroke. *I can see and smell your body rotting in your apartment!*" I do not engage her; she is ferociously trying to induce anxiety in me by projecting the ultimate threat of death. I point out that she is projecting, but she escalates the assault: "You've had such a terrible life. Such a really *terrible, terrible, terrible* life!"

I know that trick too: now she is trying to induce guilt that I've been a failure, a wretched failure, to meet all her expectations, to obey her dictates, and to give her enough gratification to boost her ego's insatiable demands.

"You've had such a terrible life. You could easily just kill yourself. *You could commit suicide!*" She's reached a crescendo and I hear the barely concealed message that I am so awful that I should kill my own self. But that too, is a projection. My mother feels suicidal and is demanding I feel the same as she, insisting, forever insisting, "We are one."

I point out that she has a morbid tone in her voice and I hope she's not depressed. "I'M NOT MORBID! I *LIVE* WITH DEATH, MICHAEL, I *LIVE* WITH DEATH!" she retorts.

"I don't like the way this conversation is going, Mom."

"Well, *neither do I!*" We hang up on each other simultaneously.

*

DON'T YOU DARE!

I have been fighting the last battle for my liberation these past two weeks; I had to reclaim my individuality from my mother's control. The war is taking a heavy toll and I'm experiencing the strangest exhaustion of my life. I let my mother simmer in her rage about my individuating away from her and about writing a book she is afraid of. Then, I called home. My father answered saying they were just fine and chatted a minute. My mother would not speak to me. I waited a few more days, and this time my mother answers the phone. I tell her that the writing is going well and how excited I am about the process of the book.

"Well, I just hope it brings in enough money to put food on your table and is not a total waste of time. I'll pray for that much," she laments. I hear instead: 'I won't pray for success, because that would make you independent of needing our help, which I still want to use to control you.'

"Well, it might well succeed. It's very original, Mom!" I state, defensively.

"I hope it doesn't succeed, if you're going to say any more about *me* in your book!"

I hesitate. I haven't told her that I've written about her in the book. She doesn't want to hear anything about the book, but she suspects I have mentioned her and feels betrayed. So, I hear instead: 'Confess! You've already done me wrong, haven't you? You've exposed me for abusing you. You have broken the commandment: *Honor thy parents!* Stop this abusive exposure of me!'

Mom emphasizes, "It better *not* draw attention to me, Michael. I'm not exactly shy, but I have, well, what one might call a *retreating* personality, you know. I'm not like *some* people who just have to get up and speak their minds in public." She talks with a pejorative tone, implying that only egotists who crave the spotlight have the disreputable behavior of public speaking. "So, if it's successful, I hope you won't talk about *me* when you speak in public!" she adds.

I feel like saying something more in my defense, but decide to keep quiet. It's best to not try to justify my right to have my own life and freedom of speech. I don't care what my mother thinks because her intentions are dishonorable. I refrain from saying: 'So, Mom, you expect it to be a failure, which is bad for me. But if it succeeds, it's bad for you. You are willing to allow me some minimal success, just enough for food on the table, but not enough to be financially self-sufficient and independent of you. No matter what comes of the book, my future is full of trouble, isn't it? I'm always going to have to depend on you and be a bad child, won't I?'

"So, how *do* you spend your time these days?" My mother sallies. I hear instead: 'Why aren't you being an obedient child and spending time with me? I need my fix of my missing dependent child. I need the state of being gratified by you.'

"Oh, I'm pretty much engrossed in writing, Mom."

"Just writing? JUST WRITING?" She snarls back contemptuously.

"Yes, Mom."

"I don't think the book will succeed at all. You're wasting your time."

"Mom, you don't have to worry so much about me. I can cope with whatever comes from the book."

"I'm not worrying! There is a difference between *worrying* and *proper planning*, Michael." I hear instead: 'You're being irresponsible and you will be punished for not doing what I want you to do.'

*

DISOWNED, DISINHERITED AND DISCREDITED

"It is a natural part of the process of healing from toxic shame and trauma that people experience a fair amount of guilt. In these first thirteen days of writing, I, too, have had haunting feelings of guilt; at moments of self-doubt, I wonder if writing about my family secrets will lead to my disinheritance and a complete rejection from my family members—earning their spite and hatred until death."
[Excerpt from my journal]

I fell for a trap set by my dysfunctional family. After a month of ever-so-slightly warming up to me and my writing project, and especially my brother's apparent wish to be more intimate, the unexpected, but not surprising, rapid-fire sequence of events that led to the extinction of my family ties took place with the dizzying speed and giddy whirlwind of a tornado.

INDIVIDUATION

*

Later, on the same evening of the restaurant event, my father calls me. He asks, "What can we do to *help* you, Michael?" I offer the idea of family counseling, with the caveat that my brother would have to be included.

Then I call my brother to enlist his cooperation.

Roy, Jr., replies, "I couldn't *bear* to dig up my childhood. My ego-strength can't handle it." He claims to be too fragile to do therapy. Besides, he argues, there are two theories about how to treat overwhelming trauma: *desensitize* it, or use every repressive defense possible to *block it out*. He states that he adheres to the latter theory. I explain that the use of such defenses leads to a shame-based personality and even Narcissism. But he holds almost hysterically onto his position.

Then, abruptly, Roy, Jr., shows interest in hearing about my writing project for the first time. I ask him if he'd like to see the original Book One, which deals with childrearing practices and my developmental years. He joyously replies, "SURE!" He seems to be supportive of my writing and to be on my side about the family issues. But he might also be enticing me into a very risky mistake.

> *"My brother loved to scare me in the forest, too. He would prod me to climb up a tall tree, nudging me from underneath—promising to catch me should I fall. When I'd reached unwieldy branches, and felt sufficiently scared, he would scamper down as fast as he could and run away—leaving me pleading for help."*

I email the book to him on Saturday, August 28th, 2010. That day will be forever remembered as the demise of my family. My brother, my only sibling, betrays me far worse than he had when he made me walk blind over the coiled rattlesnake.

He does not "read" the book; he does not "look" at any of the agonizing entries about why and how I've had to expose my family for my own survival. My brother immediately scans the book with a word search for any parts that contain "brother" or "Roy." The word "brother" comes up ninety-seven times. In sheer paranoia, he concludes that *all* of those relate to him and that he is the subject of "one hundred derogatory pages."

Roy immediately calls my parents, against my request that he not do so, and spits out the most venomous and damaging "bits" to them with *ad lib* verbal ranting. He does not read the text to them, his rendering is out of context and without mitigation, and his explicit intention is to make them jaundiced against my work. A smear campaign against me has begun, with the sole goal being to protect my family's social façades and self-images. My brother's primary intention becomes that of discrediting and invalidating my experiences, protecting his own reputation, and turning my parents finally and fully against me.

Within twenty-four hours, I speak with my *brother* for perhaps the last time in my life. He calls me, screaming, "Your book is totally fraudulent! It's filled with gross errors! You'll ruin my career! I'll sue you for libel!"

YOU'RE A LIAR!

In an instant, he both retracts his previous opinion of his own childhood trauma and he defends his lifelong cruelty toward me. "Our childhoods were *normal,* given the times. *Every* child got whipped, beaten, and threatened with death. *All* big brothers beat up, refused to support, and put the lives of their younger siblings at risk," he declares.

He reiterates these statements when we have one session together with my therapist the following week, insisting that our childhood experiences were normal and there was no abuse. My therapist, Christine, then asks him if such behavior would be considered abuse *today.* Roy looks surprised and ponders the question for a moment. He is a tenured associate professor of psychiatry at Stanford Medical School and he knows the law. He answers, "Of course, it would be considered abuse today!"

Twelve hours after speaking to my brother, I speak to my *mother* for perhaps the last time in my life. She says mournfully, "I'm dismayed by what is happening to the family. Of course, your book has ruined my reputation and I'll lose whatever friends I have left. It will cause me to have a nervous breakdown and maybe commit suicide. But I'm also very concerned about *your* mental health—how could you invent such fables?"

YOU'RE INSANE!

Twenty-four hours after speaking to my mother, I speak to my *father* for perhaps the last time in my life. He yells, "I DISOWN YOU AND I DISINHERIT YOU! You are no son of mine! And I hope you get lots of money from the book—so I can sue you for libel and take every penny away! *How dare you expose us like this?* You have no family loyalty! *You don't love us!*" Then my father hangs up.

YOU'RE A TRAITOR!

I feel simultaneously cast out of Eden and liberated from hell. I hear myself saying, 'Forgive them, Lord, for they know not what they do.' The book has unleashed the most-feared shadow side of all my family members. Their full arsenal of psychological and tactical weapons accosts me, the worst of which is complete denial that abuse ever occurred. My spiritual Self fades and my angry, adolescent, Self instantly constructs rigid boundaries of self-preservation.

Then I feel relieved.

The worst has been made manifest.

Somehow I knew all this would happen….

This segment is a piece of poetic prose about toxic parenting, with the metaphor of "the dragon" —and leading to some resolution of my internal conflict.

FINALITY

There have been twists and turns in my relationship with my parents since I last wrote about them in the Interlude. After "The Last Slap of the Paper Dragon's Tail," there were more slaps, as I knew there would be. The abuse escalated; the attacks alternated with a seductive insistence that they loved me deeply, and that the love necessitated the attacks. But each slap was thinner paper and each tail-swipe made me stronger.

The worst issue for me to cope with is "victim-abuser reversal." My parents continue to blame me, the victim, for the repercussions of their past and present abuse. "You're a failure, because you're a failure, and you abuse us, saying we abused you." The second worst thing is that they deny that abusive events ever happened, called "gas lighting."

I did not have to vanquish my parents. I did not have to slaughter the DRAGON of their possessive solipsism. I just had to change myself by writing this book. And I've also had to pull my "sub-personalities" back into action.

The dissociated child and the pre-adolescent pleaser are of no help with my family; they're used to being either passive or appeasing, which predators can bend to their will and exploit. The imperative to please them desisted for good.

Codependent patterns have devastated my entire life.

I had to regress to my angry, adolescent Self instead. I regained his presence as one of the five elements of my epiphany in the Interlude. Thanks to this part of me, I can now experience safety, security, and contentment because I have stronger boundaries than before—perhaps even with a bit of self-entitlement. He took the lead and championed the struggle for my independence from my parent's weapons of control. My parents fought back fiercely to retain their control. I went through a phase of hating and despising the DRAGON. The uncomfortable, but necessary, phase of hatred toughened my boundaries even more.

My sad subpersonality has begun the arduous process of fully grieving. I don't recall my parents ever actually listening to any of my life's experiences. When I'd insist that they "hear" me, they would always tell me I was lying or making it all up or exaggerating...Or they'd had worse experiences, or better stories. I was ignored and silenced and had to listen to their mundane woes and experiences while mine were discounted. In grief, I can accept that my wish to be known and validated by the two most significant people in my early life history may be forever thwarted.

My "*non*-shame-based" or the "love-based" part, the new fifth element among my subpersonalities, helps me reclaim faith in a positive outcome for myself. He has progressed even further, into greater compassion and nearly absolute forgiveness of the DRAGON. With his help, I am now capable and willing to take care of my parents in their final stage of life.

The strategic roles of parent-child have reversed.

With my parents' aging, and with the revelation of this very condensed and mitigated account of my life, written and destined for publication, their stature will diminish and their shame will increase. At the same time, my own stature may increase and my shame will further disappear by the simple magic of exposure: I have told my TRUTH. The power of TRUTH is much greater than the power of the DRAGON.

*

THE DRAGON LOVES ME. I held shut the castle's gates against the arrows, spears, clubs, and flames of solipsism. "You've always been more special to us than your brother. We feel closer and more attached to you, Michael. We feel a unique connection with you...I'm not sure why," my father said. "We wait for your calls! *Nobody* else's call means so much!" my mother cried out.

I know why—*solipsism*, on many, many levels. I have rebelled against their devastating emotional abuse and their engulfment of me as a house slave. Their fight for the right to keep me as a smaller, always *smaller*, subset of themselves would last until their deaths and beyond if not defied now. I have finally broken free from the prison of a dependent child state. Their narcissistic compulsion to control me has been thwarted. There are no longer hands that hold me down and hold me back, or puppet strings that make me dance for their amusement.

I went to my parents' church a few months ago, and the sermon was on "The Prodigal Son." I sat next to my mother, who constantly stared at me, shaking her head and crying through the entire service. She will always hold and cherish the image of me as a "good child turned into a prodigal son" and see themselves as "perfect parents and devoted martyrs."

'Michael's just a child, our dependent child, our good little boy who can't grow up and fend for himself. And if he does try to grow up, different from our wishes, he'll make mistakes and fail. But even when he fails, he's still our little boy, just our *bad* little boy—our prodigal son. And so, we've got to mold him, warn him, or punish him to protect him from being hurt by the world he'll never grow up to understand.'

*

THE DRAGON GUARDS A TREASURE IN ITS CAVE. I defused their weapon of "money." The threat to disinherit me did not matter; I've weathered that threat many times already, whenever I resisted their will. "All you need is our inheritance! Someday, maybe you'll get $300,000, and at 8% interest, you'll be set for the rest of your life. But you won't get the principal—*you'd squander it.*"

When I mention that I might sell the book, they reply, "What do you mean, making money by writing a book? Even if you got a million dollars, at 1% interest, you'd starve. You're much better off on *our* money!"

The biased math and flawed logic was not apparent to them.

Just before last Christmas, I asked my parents for a loan of three hundred dollars, which I used to buy gifts for them. Soon after, my parents arranged for the family to gather for the traditional holiday dining-out event, which they have always paid for. I am seated between my mother and father, which is not a comfortable position to be squeezed into. I am immediately scolded as an ungrateful wastrel in front of my brother and niece. It worked; I regressed from a fifty-five-year-old adult to a three- or six-year-old child state.

"May I have an appetizer, *please*, Dad?" I whine, beseechingly.

"Ask your mother," he replies gruffly.

"May I, Mom?" I plead.

The answer is, "**NO**." I understand and hear her message: 'You've been bad, Michael. You asked for money. You are dependent on us, as we want, but you should also be independent, as we also want.'

When appetizers arrive for everybody except me, my father decides to share his with my mother. He lifts his tray of delectable treats high up, over and past me, "over the child's head," passing the food to her. I feel horribly ashamed by the symbolic gesture. As if I would try to reach up and grab the plate like a spoiled brat.

"You can't manage at your age! It's too late for an IRA. My God, you only have five hundred dollars in an IRA."

"GET A JOB! A real job with guaranteed income! And just do whatever they tell you to do. It doesn't matter if it's unethical!"

"Michael, we just got a call and they're looking for a doctor to run a methadone clinic, only a few hours commute away. Don't you think you should be reasonable and take it?"

*

THE DRAGON'S TAIL LASHES AT MY BOOK. My parents are sophisticated, yet simple-minded. In solipsistic projection, they cannot imagine *themselves* writing a book or succeeding outside of the small familiar box of patterns that has been their life, rooted in the remote past. Since I am a clone of their egos, they cannot imagine *me* doing what I am now doing. They feel obligated to stifle my creativity and abort my baby.

"It's such a bad economy. There's no money to be gained anywhere, certainly not by writing a silly book."

"No, we don't want to read it or know anything about it. Just get it out of your system; maybe then you'll be reasonable, after your self-indulgence."

I hear my mother's jealous voice as she casts the solipsistic web. "So, the book is almost done? GOOD! You can let go of this capricious folly of squandered time and come back to your senses and look for a job." Or, even more seditious, "You can now come back to *me*, and leave my rival—that book— behind!"

Writing is not a job for them, and "to be a writer" is only role-play.

Writing is done for pleasure, so it's a pastime, a game, or a toy.

INDIVIDUATION

*

THE DRAGON IS SUPPOSED TO SCARE ME. I defused their weapon of "fear." I dismantled their paranoid worldview and I held steadfast trust in my future. My mother is very religious, but she lacks the spiritual quality of faith. Her message is the same old combo: 'You can't trust yourself because your intuition is foolish. You can't trust anybody else because they will all trick you. Therefore, you must always be very afraid and trust only us.'

For my parents, whatever is not a tangible and accomplished fact is assumed to be a foolish fantasy, due to being influenced by the treachery of others or being duped. "Your literary agent is a CROOK!" My mother becomes aggravated and hysterical, thinking I'd paid somebody to be an agent, and that I was already squandering the little inheritance I was about to receive from my great aunt's estate.

"I don't care about the damn future, MOM! I'll just let whatever happens, happen. I will let God's will and nature take its course," I shouted.

And then she changed. "Well, since you're not worried at all, and you have all that faith that things will turn out well...." I completed her sentence in my mind: 'Then, maybe, I don't have to be afraid anymore, either!'

I whispered to myself, 'You can trust your inner voice.'

Then, I told myself, 'You don't have to be afraid anymore.'

*

THE DRAGON BREATHES FIRE AND DEATH. I defused the eternal death threat, which absolutely *had* to be nullified. The threat of violent death by suicide carried no more power over me; I've let it torment and restrict my entire life. Should my mother threaten to kill herself again, I am prepared to say, "If you feel that way, Mom, you need help and you should see a therapist."

But more real, now, is the ever-imminent natural death. "We're nearly on our deathbeds and you must obey our *last wishes,* and do what we want you to do so we can rest in peace!"

My father jokes about "using the law of numerical averaging" when telling others his age. So, when he arrived at eighty-four years old, he

115

could "honestly" say, "Well, I'm *almost* eighty." He just had his 85th birthday two weeks ago. My father is now, by his law of averages, almost ninety years old. My father recently had cataract surgery. He laments, "I'll be on dialysis soon, my creatinine level keeps inching up…my chronic cough is emphysema…and my acid reflux is getting worse…."

Beliefs are stronger than omens: They can be self-fulfilling.

My mother always believed that when her aunt died, she would be next in the line of succession. Her aunt died a few months ago. My mother carries the conviction that she is now imminently close to the afterlife.

She is also convinced that she will get Alzheimer's, like her own mother had, or some other form of dementia due to brain damage. "Where is my little black book? I just can't remember much anymore…." Her voice trails off mournfully.

One can also choose to forget; "forgetfulness" can be passive aggressive or a way to manipulate others through sympathy. But my mother has *always* suffered some ailment and she has *always* been near death. "I was feeling so weak; it turned out I was taking too many pills for my diabetes."

Mom just flew back to Nashville for her college reunion. She made a point of mentioning, "There's only six of us left now—out of several hundred who graduated." When one graduates from college at age sixteen and everyone else is twenty-two, the age discrepancy means a lot. But when you're now eighty-three years old…

I feel at peace with my parents.

That is a miracle, for had I not taken on the project of writing this book, I would have never successfully grieved their loss, and I would still exist as an extension of them. Their death would have meant my death. The last time I visited my parents, I saw them differently.

There was no thunder for me, only a sigh.

My parents were just being their predictable selves.

My father would not greet me and sat in the living room. He was sulking and indignant because I'd asked him to stop berating me as soon as he picked up the phone whenever I called, and to *welcome* my calls instead. He was irate at my request that he change a simple behavior.

My mother looked extremely frail.

She exaggerated her fumbling and weakness for my benefit. She showed me pictures of deceased ancestors and rambled almost inaudibly about who was who, interlaced with frequent reminders about her poor memory. Her hands trembled and she could hardly hold the photographs.

Finally, my father came into the dining room and began to chastise me. "Now, when you get your great aunt's inheritance, after we deduct all the money you owe us, and lied saying you'd pay us back, don't go spending it all on stupid things like investments! *We* know how to invest, but it's too complicated for *you* to learn. You just can't be trusted with money…."

'I bet you can't do it!' The words were not spoken but, as always, implied. I muttered to myself, 'I have confidence in you and I'm *sure* you can do it!'

I immediately interrupted my father with a self-assured tone of voice. "I understand your concern about my financial self-sufficiency, Dad, and I'm working on it. But there are some things I want to deal with on my own." My father stopped the harangue and looked surprised. I continued, "Everything is under *my* control, Dad. You don't have to get involved. My book will be successful. Or, if not, then I'll manage to be self-sufficient some other way."

"Well, if you're so *sure* you can do it…." He became quiet.

The strategic roles of parent-child have reversed.

It's finally appropriate that I should function as their caretaker; it was not appropriate to assume that role starting at age seven. There is a genetic bond between a child and his or her parents. But loyalty to one's parents at the cost of one's own life is a horrible form of slavery. Children have a right to individuate and a duty to halt the transmission of transgenerational abuse. Exposure stops the abuse and stops the shame and stops the DRAGON.

Dad's bark has become a quiet whimper.

Mom's curse has become a soft prayer.

THE DRUMBEAT OF LIFE'S HEARTBEAT BECOMES A SLOW HEAVY ROLL

*

An invitation arrived in the mail yesterday. It was to my parent's 60th wedding anniversary, to be held at their country club in a few weeks. There will be over a hundred guests gathered to honor my mother and father. I will speak kind words about my parents there.

And perhaps, someday, they will read this book and come to know me. It doesn't matter. The most important and life-changing transition has already happened. I have a new perspective. The past is dismissed. I am free of my solipsistic wounds. I can fully let go of my parents when they die. I know that I am now capable of discerning healthy intimates. I have broken loose from the shackles, chains, ropes, and hands that hold me back.

The DRAGON of the cross-generational bondage of house slaves has now nearly died.

This medium length segment comes towards the end of my adventure of self-healing, and represents a resolution of the book's primary themes. Several anecdotes add luster, humor, suspense— and the ending is in poetic prose.

The first piece, "STOP," is a string of chilling associations about sleeping or stopping; it carries a codependent subtheme, and is characteristic of sleep terror, or *pavor nocturnus*, as well as post-traumatic stress disorder (PTSD). The joyous conclusion overshadows the initial imagery.

STOP!

The fear of stopping all began long ago with my fear of sleeping. I never slept as a child in dread of the violence that could erupt within or around my home at any time. I panted with mute terror in the initial bedtime hours, for just when my vigilance would fall, at the precise moment when I let down my guard, danger could pounce upon me unprepared.

Suddenly, the bedroom door is thrown open! Enter Ophelia, the madwoman, to whom I must plead for my life…until Dad had to start giving me Valium by age ten. I escaped the torment by staying awake, in a dissociated, dream-like state. Toward morning, I would be fully awake long before it was time to get up. Then I'd shiver with terror again, dreading going to school.

When I did fall asleep, I had nightmares.

I would be walking down endless stairs to a bottomless basement. Dungeons, wine cellars, sordid secrets and hell reside in the underworld, which is always "down there." I kept going down the stairs into a one-way abyss, with doors shutting and locking behind me after each flight.

INDIVIDUATION

My father kept the German shepherd guard dog locked up in the dimly lit, unfinished part of our basement. Dad named him "Pip"—the orphan from "Great Expectations" with a secret rich father and a cold foster mother. One of my chores was to go down to the basement and scoop up his excrement, for he rarely got to come up and go outside for a natural release. It's the same part of the basement where my father tried to tongue kiss me.

Grandma Johnson, my father's second foster mother, kept her basement locked and secret. I never knew what she hid down there. Grandma Johnson was a hillbilly version of Miss Havisham in the Charles Dickens's novel; she was stern, silent, strict, and scary. One afternoon I stood on the small front porch of her three-room farmhouse, watching her rocking slowly in her chair and gazing into her cornfield.

Suddenly, Grandma Johnson squinted and stopped rocking. She called out to my father, "ROY! Go down to the basement and bring me up my shotgun!" My father mechanically obeyed without question. Mrs. Johnson took the rusty rifle, aimed into the corn patch, and fired a shot. "ROY! Go bring me that *dead* rattlesnake!" I was petrified, seeing just one of the things she kept in her basement. I never did anything that might possibly displease Grandma Johnson.

My maternal grandmother, Evelyn Foster Holloway, also kept her basement door locked and secret. It was where she stashed all the "dirty" coins and bills she'd ever received in change after a purchase. She took the money into her white gloved hands, and then it was ritualistically carted through the mysterious basement door and dropped into huge, white, sealed laundry sacks for eternity—amounting to more than $20,000 by late life.

Being on call as a doctor intensified my sleep phobia. My entire life was punctuated by sleepless nights, night after night for many decades, and roused every half hour or so to deal with the sick souls for whom I was responsible. During my internship, the residents' sleeping quarters were located directly above the emergency room. I could hear the shrill wailing of ambulance sirens and the screams of the drug-demented, the traumatized, and the dying from the ER below my bed.

I waited in panic for my beeper to summon me "down there" into endless scenarios of blood-soaked madness and burnt or crushed bodies. Or perhaps, I'd be called to resuscitate a meconium-covered comatose preemie in the intensive care nursery.

Then the *sleeping phobia* generalized to a *stopping phobia*. Stopping meant failure in the racist and competitive world. "Keep swimming, keep running, keep working, keep achieving—there's no time for sleep." Pulling off all-nighters began in fifth grade and intensified in prep school and college. It was quasi-normal in the high-pressure schools I attended.

As I became an out-of-control codependent, stopping came to mean *failure* —by giving up and finally ending an abusive situation, or calling off a rescue search. During the relationship or job, I would work incessantly, cleaning and beautifying the home, or pouring over patient's charts and researching treatment plans, until late at night.

"I haven't done enough to *please* everybody, yet"

"I haven't done enough to *rescue* everybody, yet!"

INDIVIDUATION

I arrived at the extreme that I could only sleep with a partner, *any* partner. When they slept in bed with me, I felt both *safe* —because of their company, and *relieved* — given a moratorium from their torment.

The drop in my tension allowed me to get some sleep at last.

When the abusive relationship or job ended, I would go through an emotional withdrawal that was worse than any chemical detox I can imagine. I would rack my mind, searching for 'Why?' and questioning my behavior, looking for my fault as my mother had taught me to do. Somehow, I always arrived at the agonizing conclusion: 'I was bad.'

And bad people go to hell…

And hell is an exile to *down there*…

And I go *down there* when I stop, fail, or fall asleep…

Then the *sleeping, stopping,* and *failure* phobias came to symbolize *death.* I learned that stasis of cell growth is the definition of medical death. Like most physicians, stopping and stasis and stagnation and death all blended together. My fear of stopping and sleeping generalized to dying even more when I began to suffer depression. I shifted from: Now I lay me down to sleep, and if I die before I wake…To sleeping all day in depressed misery wishing I were dead.

When I indulged in alcohol and tranquilizers to help with my depression and trauma, falling asleep often meant that I would awaken dehydrated and in a state of acute withdrawal after a blackout. I waited with bated breath in the twilight before morning, until the hour when the liquor store would open—tremulous hours of fretting and wondering what damage did I do in my blackout?

Or, 'Whom did I call? What did I say?'

Eventually, my fear of falling asleep, stopping, and death became a massive tangle of traumatic imprints, accumulated little moments of hell that grew to haunt the core of my soul, until: "I pray the Lord my soul to take." The only way to survive was to keep constantly busy and never sleep or stop at all.

*"I **LIVE** WITH DEATH, MICHAEL. I **LIVE** WITH DEATH!"*
My mother screams.

Serenity…security…surrender…sleep… The four states are joined like a quadruplet of sisters. Sleep does not mean danger or failure or death anymore. My fear of slowing down and stopping has nearly been overcome. Stasis does not necessarily mean death; it can also mean the end of an old cycle.

Here is my summary resolution of my quest for identity and the process of individuation—found in the Afterword of "Hide and Play Dead."

INDIVIDUATION

During the process of writing "Hide and Play Dead," I retraced the dissection of my identity into internal subpersonalities and external social roles. The challenge was to create a Self that could solve the riddle of being *both* extraordinary and ordinary.

The first solution was to simply identify with an extraordinary peer group, as my elitist education provided; there, I could fit in as an *ordinary member of an extraordinary group*. But the opportunity to maintain such an identity faded after college, and such an elitist self-image restricts one to an unreal and dangerously narcissistic worldview.

The second solution evolved slowly: It was to accept the marginated status of an *outside observer with no defined group identity* at all. And, like any researcher, scientist or philosopher, that is how I have gained much of my life's wisdom.

The third solution to the riddle of ordinary-extraordinary was the most painful, that of an *in-between*. It meant accepting myself with *neither a group nor a fixed personal identity*, like a mural of composite pieces borrowed from many origins.

In any one of the three options for individuation—by "communion with extraordinary people," as an "observer," or as an "in-between" — I can finally enjoy my unique gifts and claim my liberation from the ancestral riddles of slavery. I could not fit in, I could not conform, and—thanks to a colossal series of mismatches and contradictions—I was never fully branded in any decisive way at all!

I moved to a little town called Yountville, in the Napa Valley of northern California, when I was in my mid-twenties. I quickly sought out the company of local gays, and they looked at me in shock. "You're black, gay, *and* intelligent? Wow. You're going to have a terribly tough time here. You can only be *two out of the three* to survive. Black, gay, and dim-witted will do; gay, intelligent, and white is OK; black, intelligent, and straight is adequate." My advisors were right then and still right today—in all but the most eclectic and avant-garde communities in the United States.

My early experience of racial ostracization freed me from peer and community "signatures." Later, to be rejected by the black community fully blocked me from adopting a racial identity whatsoever. I even tried to be Jewish, but fortunately I failed. To be gay freed me from conscription into gender stereotypes and allowed my psychic empathy to flourish. To be rejected by most of the gay community because of racism kept me from adopting a stereotypical gay identity. To be educated by the elite, but without the status or membership within the private club of white elitism, kept me from adopting a class identity. To enter a field that lacked congruence with my deepest interests kept me from adopting a professional identity as a standard doctor and becoming a member of the "Guild of Gentlemen Physicians."

It's always been easy for people to tag me as "it" — the outsider, the different one, no matter how hard I try to fit in. My vague and un-stamped identity was out of the ballpark: *black, gay, intellectual, elite,* and finally, *non-conformist physician.* It's almost as if these marks that are lightly branded on my brain are noticed by others in a primal and instinctual manner. The five aspects of my identity confound other people and they lead to restricted choices in relationships, friendships, and peer group acceptance.

But I've been used to rejection and even violent repudiation since I was six years old. There is virtually no ordinary group in existence in America to which such a composite identity pertains. The crude realization is that I just represent too many non-ordinary features. Ninety-nine percent of social groups will allow only *two* of the *five* out-lying standard identities, maximum, to be able to still squeeze in on the margin of commonality.

Each of these standard identities is pushed even further toward the margin by sub-typing. I'm too straight acting to be gay, too sensitive to be straight. I'm too white to be black, too black to be white. I'm too poor to join the ruling class, too educated to join the working class. I'm too worldly to be a doctor, too much of a healer to be a diplomat.

Sometimes, the wrong mix of just *two* marks is sufficient ground for rejection. Black and gay will not mix because the gay community is twice as racist as the straight, and the black community is the most homophobic of all ethnic groups in the country. Doctor and Harvard will not mix; interactions with fellow physicians are tainted by professional envy because of Harvard.

People who are both different and gifted have two basic choices. They can hide in shame, passively marginalized outside of the mainstream of life—perhaps ignored as eccentric or crazy. Or they can courageously stand out, assume active leadership as a role model—an icon for a new way of being—perhaps even respected as a pioneer or genius.

Historically, crazy and genius do seem to go together quite well.

The curse of my ancestral past and the lack of a fixed identity transform into a blessing: It has lead me to a psychospiritual breakthrough as I wrote this book. I was not marked for enslavement and subservience to conformity, as were my ancestors. To have an independent identity violates the caveat of the house slave or obedient field slave, although, before writing this book, being a submissive codependent seemed quite natural. To strive for excellence, but not status saturated with narcissistic qualities, curtails the role of the rebellious field slave or freed light-complexioned house slave.

Apparently, I was created for a different destiny, one flowing naturally from a free and unique, non-slave Self. I realize that I have no choice but to pave my own path once again, but on a much larger scale than my small private practice. I call this bold milepost and the audacity to write books such as these my "grandstand time." At the least, it replaces my lost wish of becoming a grandfather. My legacy is through the creation of a new generation of thought, and not by the procreation of a new generation of offspring.

There is a fourth option for my truest identity. Perhaps now I must become a leader, especially when being a follower breaches my moral integrity. I've avoided being a leader my whole life. Perhaps I already am a leader, for I have been a role model for thousands of people and professionals who look to me for guidance.

I have no regrets.

In retrospect, I am so very glad that my quest for a registered brand of social identity was lost. I would not have discovered so much about shame without suffering rejection and alienation. Because my fragments of Self were so much at odds with each other inside of me and at odds with common social markings outside of me, I have a blessed fortune: At age fifty-eight, I can still sail or steam forward in a completely different "identity-ship."

Michael King, MD is a graduate from both Harvard College and Harvard Medical School and he has had over four decades of experience in healthcare and communication skills. His love for biopersonality, consciousness, neuropsychiatry and international health prepared him to explore the essence of human nature.

He specialized in mind-body therapy in his alternative practice, and he has also worked in virtually all aspects of conventional medicine. He is currently a pioneer in social engineering and the first physician to address shame and social oppression, pinpoint their psychobiological roots, and invent treatment programs to resist them.

Dr. King is an expert in writing technology, listening skills, and public speaking, so writing a multi-genre, memoir-driven novel, "Hide and Play Dead," came as naturally as his self-help professional literature in "Overcoming Oppression."

Michael currently has a private practice in psychotherapy and psychiatry in Desert Hot Springs, California where he specializes in the treatment of shame, abuse, trauma, and social oppression. His treatment process is based on high empathy, high rapport, client-centered approaches, along with somatic therapy and non-invasive emerging technologies in the neurosciences.

His current writing project is a study manual and workbook to accompany "Overcoming Oppression." A guide to his treatment system for healthcare professionals will soon follow—representing a paradigm shift for most of the social sciences and the field of medicine.

"It is time for the healer to emerge from the walls of clinical medicine and tackle the social milieu where illness is perpetuated. It is time for a new and revolutionary branch of medicine to take a stand against the primary source of human suffering in the world today."